# THE
# CHANGING FACE
# OF LUTON

## An Illustrated History

Stephen Bunker
Robin Holgate
Marian Nichols

The
Book
Castle

Dedicated to the memory
of John G. Dony, M.B.E., Ph.D., Hon. F.L.S.,
botanist and historian

First published April 1993
by
The Book Castle
12 Church Street
Dunstable
Bedfordshire LU5 4RU

ISBN 1 871199 71 9 (paperback)
ISBN 1 871199 66 2 (hardback)

Computer Typeset by Keyword, Aldbury, Hertfordshire.
Printed in Great Britain by the Alden Press, Oxford

# Contents

# Acknowledgements

This book was designed to complement two exhibitions which were mounted at Luton Museum and Art Gallery in November 1992 and at the Stockwood Craft Museum in April 1993. It includes a number of photographs from the vast collections of the Luton Museum Service and the Luton News, many of which have not been published before. The original photographs, representing the diverse elements of local life through the years, varied not only in content but also in quality. The clarity with which they are reproduced on the pages of this volume is testimony to the skill and patience of the Museum's Photographer, Chris Grabham, who originally joined the Museum Service in 1986 on an M.S.C. scheme and since has joined as a full-time member of staff. The line drawings and the artist's views of Waulud's Bank, Puddlehill and Luton market were produced by Jo Richards. Thanks are due to Mark McCall, the Museum's Documentation Officer, and to Rosemary Grabham and Carolyn Wingfield, Keeper of Archaeology at Bedford Museum, for reading through the text and making a number of helpful and valid comments.

*Luton's Electricity Station, taken from Crescent Road at dusk on 19 November 1956. This was built upon the site of St. Mary's vicarage. (Reproduced with kind permission of Eric Meadows.)*

# Introduction

Luton is very much a 20th-century success story, recording a population which tripled between 1901 and 1951 on the back of rapidly expanding engineering industries which took root in the town in the early 1900s. This growth was sustained during the inter-war period when the town became a magnet for migrating workers, many of whom came from the depressed regions of Britain. Luton had become transformed from a small market town to a busy industrial and commercial centre.

The town lies in the heart of the north Chilterns, a region officially designated as an Area of Outstanding Natural Beauty, and it provides a stark contrast with the surrounding rolling downland which is well suited for arable and livestock farming. The town has grown from this rural community but its

*Joey Dancer's Farm on Bradgers Hill in 1903*

7

development in the last 170 years has been at a rate so prodigious as to outstrip all other towns in the region. In 1821, for example, Luton bore much in common with nearby Leighton Buzzard, both being market towns in the straw plaiting region of the south-east midlands with approximately equal populations (2,986 and 2,749 respectively): 40 years later Luton was four times the size of its neighbour. Other towns which were larger than Luton in 1821, such as Hemel Hempstead and Hitchin, were barely half its size in 1871. In national terms, during the latter part of the 19th and the first half of the 20th centuries, only Coventry, a city with a similar economic experience, amongst comparable places has had a rate of population increase greater than that for Luton.

The reasons for this phenomenal expansion are many and debatable; the abundance of affordable land, the availability of labour and the nature of the regional economy have all had a part to play. From its position where the Icknield Way ridgeway track forded the River Lea to an international airport on the main London to Sheffield railway line and adjacent to the M1 motorway, Luton has at times benefited from excellent communications. Whilst helping to maintain growth communications have not been responsible primarily for Luton's expansion; indeed, the most significant phases have occurred when neighbouring towns have possessed equal or even superior networks of their own. In 1769 Arthur Young complained 'If the Earl of Bute's park at Luton Hoo was not an inducement, there certainly could be none to visit that town: Notwithstanding the wretched roads I was forced to crawl through'. It was not until 1784 that the present road to Dunstable was opened and a further half century elapsed before a new Bedford road was established. Until such times journeys were long and difficult, being made by winding lanes across hills. Until 1858, the year that Luton finally acquired a railway line, Dunstable's communication network was definitely better than Luton's and even though it lost its passenger rail link with Luton (and London) in 1965 the quality of Dunstable's road links with the capital ensures that it possesses only a marginally inferior transport network to its large neighbour.

*The goods yard of Luton's Midland Railway Station c.1910. During the 1890s the railway companies used over 40 drays to deliver empty crates to Luton's hat factories each morning, returning to collect the full crates for delivery back to the stations at six in the evening. By half past six a queue of large railway company drays, smaller private drays and even men and boys carrying individual boxes, could be strung out along Bute Street from the gates of the station.*

Aylesbury, Bedford, Bletchley, Hemel Hempstead and Leighton Buzzard were amongst a number of local towns which obtained a railway link ahead of Luton during the Railway Mania which peaked in the 1840s. There were numerous reasons for Luton's failure at this time: inability to overcome the Marquess of Bute's opposition to a line crossing his land, failure to agree upon the site of a Luton station and failure to agree whether to dissect the Moor with a proposed line. Even when a scheme finally proved to be successful, through the formation of the Luton, Dunstable and Welwyn Junction Railway Company, there was an insufficient take up of shares at a key stage in the work and it took decisive intervention from the Luton branches of two banks, Sharples and Co. and the London and County (managed by Quakers Edward Lucas and William Bigg respectively), for the fulfilment of the project. Swiftly absorbed into the Great Northern Railway Company, Luton's new railway link was followed in 1868 by the opening of a second station to serve the more substantial line laid out by the Midland Railway Company which also provided the town with a more direct link with London. Both of these provided immediate benefit to the town, reducing the cost of the import of coal and straw plait and providing an export route for Luton's hats. The important point to make is that the establishment of a railway line followed Luton's predominance as the manufacturing centre for straw hats and was not its begetter. Similarly, the presence of the two railway lines,

*The Carnegie Library on the corner of Williamson Street and George Street. Opened in 1910, the Carnegie was originally able to hold over 40,000 volumes and served the town until 1962. Built by T & E Neville and designed by local architectt Basil Deacon, the Carnegie Library contained marble floors and oak panels. Its hasty demolition soon after the opening of the new Library has been to the regret of most Lutonians.*

although important, was not the decisive reason behind the arrival of the of engineering firms in the early 20th century.

The fabric of the town, for good or otherwise, and the character of its inhabitants is a congenital product of Luton's industrial heritage. The framework for the town's commercial development, established by the action (or inaction) of successive local authorities have given maximum scope for economic enterprise at the expense of features which other places would place as a higher priority, such as town planning or building conservation. This apparent commitment to little else other than ruthless change in pursuit of wealth in fact disguises a number of recurring themes in Luton's history. It may be of some consolation for present Lutonians, and perhaps instructive for planners, to discover that its perceived defects are hardly new. Those who regret the demolition of the elegant Carnegie Library in 1962 would perhaps sympathise with those who unsuccessfully opposed the destruction of Luton's ancient vicarage in 1899 (in order to make way for the electricity station) and those who lamented the disappearance of Seven Acres after 1859 with its meadows, gardens and gentle river beneath John Street, Waller Street, Bute Street, Cheapside, Silver Street and Melson Street. A century later many of these streets in turn gave way to the Arndale Centre, a shopping complex compromised far beyond its original plan. Those who complain that Luton has no history because it is always sweeping away the physical reminders of its past are in some senses missing an essential point: this record of wholesale demolition is an integral part of Luton's heritage.

The vastness of Vauxhall's presence within the town also disguises the fact that much of Luton's industrial past has been shaped by the efforts of small to medium scale entrepreneurs in construction, hat manufacture, engineering and retail. Luton has no experience of powerful individuals or companies who have exerted a deliberate influence over the town, such as Charles Palmer in Reading or H. O. Wills in Bristol, through the provision of parks, concert halls and the like or through determining the nature of land development. As the Marquess of Bute turned his attention to investment in

Cardiff from the 1840s his land holding around the centre of Luton was sold off for virtually unrestricted freehold development; the Crawley estate diminished in almost the same way during the 20th century. Vauxhall Motors, for all its contribution to the town's character and wealth, has been a company whose control lay elsewhere and whose interest in Luton was restricted to its employees and their families.

The determination of Luton's physical make-up by small entrepreneurs has been of profound influence, especially in that no one person or institution has been in a position to take an all-encompassing strategic view of the development of the town. There have been many plans, of course, and the New Industries Committee formed in the 1890s was successful beyond the belief of any of its members in attracting new firms, but the decisive imperative has primarily been a good return upon speculative investment. This has been most vividly demonstrated in the shabby muddle that the centre of the town has become. Borough Council efforts for rejuvenation

*The building of the Arndale Centre was the result of an attempt to rationalise Luton's town centre. This combined pedestrianised shopping with a series of ring roads designed to ease the congestion in streets. These had not been built to accommodate the nature and volume of traffic which, by the late 1950s, was choking them. A proposal to pedestrianise Waller Street was later replaced by one which covered the area with a purpose-built shopping centre. The original plans (1966) included residential flats and an entertainment centre but did not envisage the precinct being closed at night.*

have been hampered by its limited property holding within the town which has significantly reduced its leverage.

It is easy to identify the town centre as a problem area, being one which encapsulates Luton's difficulties with its self-esteem as a whole. Identifying a reason for this and formulating a remedy is less simple. For the resident there are, in fact, numerous outlets for recreation and enjoyment based around Luton's sporting clubs and facilities, its community centres, drama groups, religious organisations, ethnic groupings and so on. Commitment and affection dies there, however, personified not only in the dismal town centre but also in the low attendances at Luton Town F. C.'s unambitious stadium which has been wholly inadequate for the team's occassionally more exalted status. The central area has often been perceived as a problem and because of this the solution which has frequently been offered up is a civic centre, an ubiquitous panacea which has appeared as the pivotal theme in a number of plans wedged into every conceivable potential space. There have been numerous plans for rejuvenation but their repeated failure are testimony to an inability to grasp the consequence of Luton's heritage; its amalgam of individuals, companies and communities, each of which possesses its own priorities and commitments. These groups have no vested interest in a depopulated central area over which they are unable to wield positive influence.

Uncomplimentary descriptions of the town, frequently made by people who are not familiar with the place, are also not recent. Luton has, in turn, been described as a 'dirty town' (1782), a 'poor town (which) evinced marks of decadency' (1828) and a place where 'no lady dares walk the streets after dark' (1846) descriptions which can be compared with the contemporary assessment that Luton is 'an urban smudge amid the green of Bedfordshire' (1989). Although less fortunate than other towns in that it lacks distinctive features for example a harbour, cathedral, ancient university and peculiar social customs, Luton has traditionally possessed a handful of key virtues as well as being blessed by the absence of certain negative ones. Although now pushing its housing to the limits of the borough boundary, Luton has enjoyed an abundance of building ground at vital junctures in its history. This has meant more than merely the provision of homes for those migrating to the town and profits for the developers who speculated upon it: the town's housing stock, if not architectually exciting, is overall of good quality constructed in compact but not crowded streets and, most importantly of all, the houses have been affordable to the wages which were available locally. There are no slums in Luton, indeed there never were on the scale of bigger towns such as Nottingham; what bad housing did exist was mostly removed in clearance programmes in the 1930s. The open spaces within the town, although from a historic as well as a contemporary viewpoint not abundant, are varied, well maintained and have been augmented in 1992 by a Nature Conservation Strategy. Enormous potential remains within the town but, as the subsequent chapters will indicate, there are ominous signs ahead: the prerequisites of economic expansion which Luton has enjoyed in the past, such as abundant land and cheap rates, are no longer present. Even though Luton has never been a planned town in the manner, say, of Letchworth, Stevenage or Milton Keynes, it has traditionally enjoyed the mechanisms for determining its own future. The clumsy intrusion of central government in all corners of local life have removed this potential without, as yet, providing anything of benefit.

This book traces the fortunes of the settlement and economy of Luton since the earliest recorded arrival of people to the headwaters of the River Lea over 100,000 years ago and attempts to provide some answers and perhaps raise more questions about the history of this intriguing, enigmatic town. Nearly 30 years have elapsed since the last overall account of Luton's heritage, *The Story of Luton*, by Frank Stygall, James Dyer and John Dony which was subsequently revised twice. The purpose of *The Changing Face of Luton* is to augment *The Story of Luton* and the *History of Luton and its Hamlets* (1928) by William Austin (and Joseph Hight Blundell) by bringing to bear the results of more recent research which will be included in the extensive bibliography at the end of the book.

# THE EARLY YEARS

## The Earliest Inhabitants

Until 10,000 years ago, much of Britain was in the grip of the Ice Age. For nearly a million years, four ice sheets spread southwards over much of central and southern England, moulding the landscape trapped under the ice. The last time Luton was covered by an ice sheet was when the second (the Anglian) ice sheet reached as far south as London over 500,000 years ago. However, during each of the two subsequent glaciations, the Chilterns were subjected to periods of intensely cold temperatures when the frozen ground hardly thawed. Once the temperature started to rise, large quantities of water were released by the ice sheets, increasing the volume of water flowing through the major river valleys. The much swollen river in the upper stretches of the Lea valley around Luton eroded back the valley sides to the present day escarpment between Blows and Dallow Downs and the slopes between Warden and Hart Hills. As a result, a range of water-borne, glacial and wind-blown deposits accumulated within the valley and on the surrounding downland plateau.

In the late 19th century, the brickearths in and around Luton were being dug for clay to make bricks. Much of what is known today of the earliest inhabitants in Luton is due to Worthington G. Smith's diligent search of the brickpits being worked at this time. Smith, who had retired to Dunstable after working as an architectural illustrator in London, had a passion for history and local antiquities. He would walk up to 26 miles a day to visit the various brickpits around Luton for

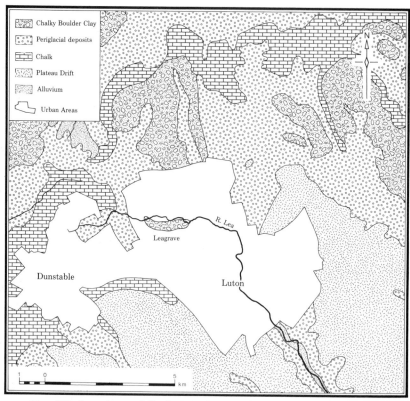

*Simplified geology of the Luton district. (Drawn by Jo Richards.)*

archaeological remains. Following his discovery in the early 1890s of humanly-struck flints in a brickpit at Caddington, he went on to recover similar material from the east Luton pits at Round Green, Ramridge End and Mixes Hill. The flints represent the remains of sites where the first people to arrive in Luton had camped for a few days and worked locally-available flint into tools that could be used for hunting and butchering wild animals. These camps had been located on the edge of ponds, a number of which occurred on the brickearths around the upper Lea valley during the Ice Age. Pollen from the site at Caddington shows that these ponds were surrounded by a narrow band of grassland which gave

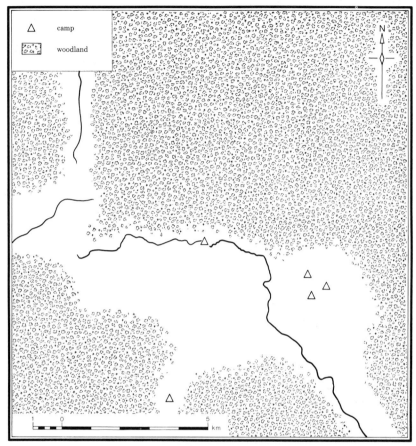

*Settlement of the Luton district, 125,000 years ago.*
*(Drawn by Jo Richards.)*

way abruptly to dense deciduous forest dominated by oak. It is likely that these sites were overnight or short-stay camps for a small hunting band of people who roamed up river valleys and through the forest hunting game and gathering natural plant foods. The type of flint tools produced and the pollen evidence suggest that these sites were occupied during the warm period before the last (the Devensian) glaciation, about 125,000 years ago.

## The last hunters

After the last glaciation, around 10,000 years ago, much of Britain was colonised by birch-pine woodland. Initially joined to the European continent by a land bridge stretching from East Anglia to south-east England, Britain was occupied by bands of hunters who used the bow and arrow to hunt mainly horse, deer and elk.

By 6,500 BC, Britain became separated from the rest of Europe by the English Channel and was covered in thick

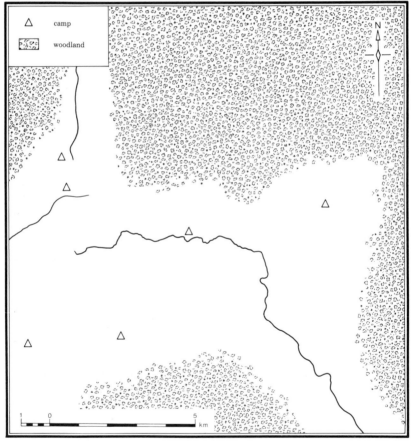

*Settlement of the Luton district, 4-7,000 BC. (Drawn by Jo Richards.)*

deciduous forest. Several hunting camps dating to this period have been found in and around Luton. At Waulud's Bank, on the eastern bank of the River Lea by Leagrave Marsh, flint tools have been found which include the tips of arrowheads and wood- and leather-working implements. These are the remains of a settlement occupied probably in the spring, summer and autumn months. On Blows Downs and on the ridge north of Stopsley further groups of flint tools have been collected which represent the remains of short-stay hunting camps, probably used in the winter months when it was easier to wander through the woodland in search of deer, wild cattle and wild pig.

## The first farmers

Sometime after 4,000 BC the concept of growing cereals and keeping domesticated animals had been introduced to Britain from the European continent. Farming communities soon established themselves on the chalk hills in southern England and the Chilterns was no exception. Areas of woodland were cleared and both farmsteads and ceremonial monuments were built. Flint tools representing farmsteads dating to this time have been found at several sites on the downs near Luton and at Pen Hill, immediately north of Waulud's Bank, Leagrave. Associated with this period are the henge monuments built throughout Britain, of which Stonehenge in Wiltshire is the best example. Waulud's Bank, the only known henge monument in the Chilterns, was built 2,500–2,000 BC near Leagrave Marsh around one of the springs feeding the River Lea. The monument consists of a D-shaped area, 18 acres (7 hectares) in extent, enclosed by an earth bank and external ditch, over 2 metres deep and 5 metres wide, with the ditch being dug to provide the material for the bank's construction. Waulud's Bank was located at the crossroads of the north Chilterns: just north of where the ridgeway route, known as the Icknield Way, forded the River Lea. By analogy with other henges there might have been large circular wooden structures within the enclosure. The monument was probably a meeting

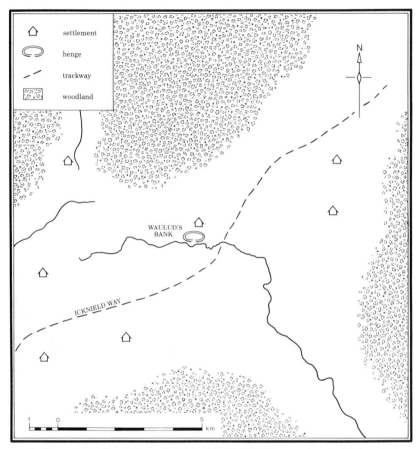

*Settlement of the Luton district, 2,500 BC. (Drawn by Jo Richards.)*

place where various ceremonies and religious gatherings could be held for residents in the Luton district and elsewhere in the Chilterns.

The first use of metal tools, initially comprising copper axes and daggers which had been imported from Europe, became widespread in Britain around 2,000 BC. In addition, the practice of burying the dead under circular earthen mounds known as round barrows came into fashion. Not everyone was buried in this way: very few children, for example, appear to

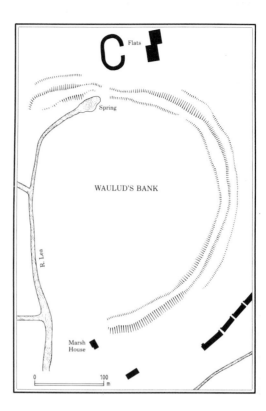

*Plan of Waulud's Bank,
Leagrave. (Drawn by
Jo Richards.)*

have been buried under round barrows in the north Chilterns, suggesting that only people of a certain status or rank received this form of burial. There are two groups of round barrows in the Luton district: the Five Knolls on Dunstable Downs and the group situated in the vicinity of Galley Hill and the Barton Hills. Excavations at both groups of barrows have recovered cremations placed in pottery urns and inhumations. One of the barrows on Galley Hill and the northernmost of the Five Knolls barrows were also used as inhumation burial sites in the late Romano-British period. The various farmsteads on the downs around Luton and at Pen Hill continued to be occupied during this period. The people buried in the barrows are thus likely to have lived in farmsteads that were mostly intervisible with the

21

*Artist's view of how Waulud's Bank appeared soon after it had been built. (Drawn by Jo Richards.)*

barrows. Excavation of three ploughed-out barrows at Bartonhill Cutting when the Barton Bypass was constructed produced evidence that the land around the barrows was rough grassland grazed seasonally. It is likely that cultivated fields surrounded each farmstead, with the land beyond being used for rough pasture.

By 700 BC, the use of iron for manufacturing a wide range of metal tools and weapons was established throughout Britain. The earlier farmsteads mentioned above had been abandoned or replaced by new settlements and the Icknield Way had become a major routeway linking East Anglia with central southern England. Mixed farming, involving the cultivation of spring-sown cereals and the management of cattle, sheep and pigs, was practised by largely self-sufficient households who occupied farmsteads that, in the Luton district, were located either side of the Icknield Way. The total

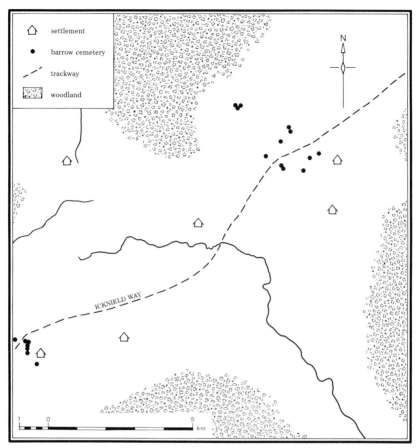

*Settlement of the Luton district, 2,000 BC. (Drawn by Jo Richards.)*

excavation of Puddlehill by the Manshead Archaeological Society of Dunstable, a farmstead situated north of Houghton Regis, gives an idea of the nature of one of these farmsteads. The main farmhouse was circular in plan and consisted of a timber framework, the walls of which had been covered in daub, topped with a conical-shaped thatched roof. Alongside was situated an outdoor hearth and a small, rectangular building which probably served as a store for grain or straw. Every 50–100 years, as the farm buildings started to decay, a

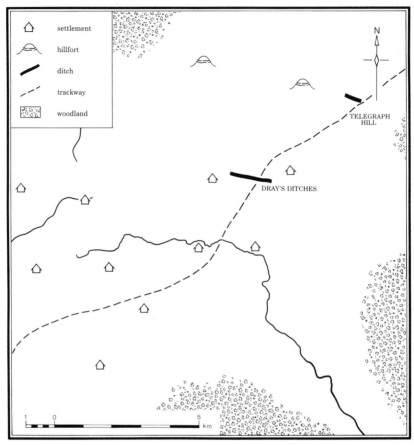

*Settlement of the Luton district before the Roman Conquest.
(Drawn by Jo Richards.)*

new farmstead was constructed up to 100 metres away. Inside
the circular farmhouse there would have been a central hearth
and oven where food was cooked, with the rest of the interior
providing a sleeping area and a space where equipment could
be stored and craft activities undertaken, for example weaving
and bone working. Additional craft activities undertaken by
each household probably included blacksmithing and making
pots for storing, processing and cooking food. Between 350

*Artist's view of the late prehistoric farmstead at Puddlehill, Houghton Regis: Top, 650–400 BC; Middle, 350–100 BC; Bottom, 100BC – AD50. (Drawn by Jo Richards.)*

and 100 BC the farmstead, comprising up to three circular buildings, was enclosed by a bank and ditch which was roughly rectangular in plan. This might have been to afford some measure of defence against feuding neighbours. That warfare between neighbouring communities took place at this time is demonstrated not only by the manufacture of iron swords and other weapons but also by the presence of fortified enclosures along the Chiltern scarp. There are four of these enclosures, known as hillforts, relatively close to Luton: Ivinghoe Beacon, Maiden Bower, Sharpenhoe Clappers and Ravensburgh Castle. It is likely that these hillforts were in use from about 700 to at least 100 BC as places of refuge and centralised stores for seed grain and other produce that could easily be defended during times of strife.

There are no known farmsteads of this period within Luton itself, the closest being those around Sundon and to the south-east of Galley Hill. All these sites are situated close to the Icknield Way. This routeway was intersected between Luton and Royston by a series of linear earthworks. These consist of one or more banks or ramparts with ditches either side that run for up to 1 km. either side of the Icknield Way. One of these sets of earthworks is Dray's Ditches, on the northern boundary of Luton, with the next series of earthworks to the north-east of Luton at Telegraph Hill. At Dray's Ditches itself, there were three V-shaped ditches, each about 2 metres deep and over 4 metres wide, with a timber-framed rampart running along the berm between the two northernmost ditches. Although their function is uncertain, these earthworks could have served as boundaries between neighbouring communities and as a means of controlling traffic along the Icknield Way.

## Before the Romans

In 55 and 54 BC, Julius Caesar led Roman military expeditions to Britain. His written account of these expeditions and the writings of other classical authors provide a picture of society in Britain before the Roman conquest in AD43. At this time Britain was inhabited by a number of tribes, each occupying a discrete geographical area. The political control of these tribes lay in the hands of a relatively small group of wealthy families who received tribute from the rest of the population in the form of farming produce and labour, the latter including service as warriors to take part in battles with neighbouring tribes when the occasion arose. At the time of Caesar's visit to Britain south Bedfordshire came under the territory of the Hertfordshire-based tribe known as the Catuvellauni, whose leader was Cassivellaunus. After making his way from the south coast and crossing the River Thames into Hertfordshire with his army, Caesar records that he attacked the Catuvellauni at Cassivellaunus' stronghold, which was well-fortified and protected by forests and marshes. Although often interpreted as being near Wheathampstead, it has been suggested that the Catuvellaunian stronghold was the Ravensburgh Castle hillfort. Caesar, after defeating the Catuvellauni and agreeing peace terms, then left Britain in the command of the tribal leaders.

In the intervening years before the arrival of the Roman army again in AD43, the Luton district continued to be part of the territory of the Catuvellauni. After the death of Cassivellaunus, Tasciovanus became leader; he established a new tribal capital at St Albans and was the first king to mint coins.

Tasciovanus' successor was Cunobelinus who, reigning from about AD10–40, extended the kingdom of the Catuvellauni to cover much of southern and central Britain. He moved the tribal capital from St Albans to Colchester. Gold and silver coins minted by Cunobelinus at Colchester have been found at Leagrave and Puddlehill.

During this period, trade with the Roman Empire intensified. The main exports were corn, cattle, gold, silver, iron, hides, slaves, hunting dogs and woollen cloaks, with the chief imports being Italian wine, fish sauces, olive oil, metal and pottery tableware, glassware and jewellery. Most of the imported goods, though, were acquired by the nobility. The head of each wealthy family received burial in style: their cremated remains were placed in a grave along with a variety of luxury items, including imported pottery vessels, shale vessels, bronze mirrors, bronze cauldrons and wooden buckets and chests with ornate enamelled bronze mounts. Burials of this nature have been found relatively near to Luton at Baldock, Harpenden and St Albans. At the other end of the social scale, the cremated remains of individuals from peasant households were buried in wheel-thrown pottery urns in designated cemeteries. One such cemetery, containing at least seven cremation burials, was uncovered at Rosslyn Crescent in Luton when houses were built there in 1962; the cemetery was probably associated with a nearby farmstead. The farmstead at Puddlehill continued to be occupied during this period, consisting of two dwellings surrounded by a series of ditched paddocks. The fill of some of these ditches produced considerable quantities of cattle bones, suggesting that cattle ranching formed part of the farming economy. Herding cattle, being less labour intensive than cultivating cereals, would have enabled farmers to spend time on active service for the nobility. Other farmsteads around Luton are known to have been situated either side of the Icknield Way. Apart from a settlement somewhere near Rosslyn Crescent, other sites of habitation in Luton itself were discovered during post-1950s housing development at Lewsey and Leagrave, the latter being situated at a fording point of the River Lea.

## Roman settlement

When Cunobelinus died in about AD40, his territory was split between his two sons, Togodumnus and Caratacus. The decisive battle of the Roman invasion in AD43 was fought at the mouth of the River Medway, where Togodumnus was killed and Caratacus fled to western Britain. Emperor Claudius then travelled to Colchester to receive the surrender of the Catuvellauni and the other tribes in southern and eastern England. From Colchester, the 14th legion marched north-westwards through Bedfordshire to conquer the Midlands, constructing a network of temporary forts and roads. One of the first major roads to be laid was Watling Street, which ran along the route of the present-day A5 from London through St Albans towards Leicester. Towns were also constructed close to each tribal capital to serve as administrative centres for collecting taxes, the nearest town to Luton being Verulamium (St Albans). Verulamium consisted of a grid pattern of streets fronted by timber-built dwellings and workshops, along with a series of public buildings constructed out of flints, tiles and mortar; these included an administrative building, a market place, a theatre, temples and the public baths. Each town, as today, had its own citizens, shopkeepers, tradespeople and administrators.

Following the creation of a network of new roads and major towns by the Romans, small market towns were established on major routeways. At Dunstable, on the intersection of Watling Street with the Icknield Way, the settlement which became known as Durocobrivis developed as a trading centre for local farmers, craftspeople and merchants to sell their wares.

Apart from the construction of roads and the foundation of towns, changes in economy and society came about through the payment of taxes to the Roman Empire. Taxes had to be paid in Roman currency; thus in order to raise money to pay taxes, goods had to be sold. Initially, farming continued as the mainstay of the economy but soon specialist craftspeople emerged, for example metalworkers and potters, operating from workshops in or near to towns and trading their wares in town shops or in the market place. The major towns were the main centres for administering the collection of taxes but it is possible that the smaller market towns also served as local collection centres. Thus the Luton district might have been administered from Dunstable rather than directly from St Albans. In Luton, the farmsteads at Leagrave and Rosslyn Crescent continued to be occupied, and the discovery of a small cemetery of at least four cremations in early Romano-British pottery urns at Richmond Hill in 1926 suggests the presence of an adjacent farmstead at Round Green. The Boudican revolt, an uprising against the Roman army in AD60–61 led by Boudica, Queen of the Iceni tribe in

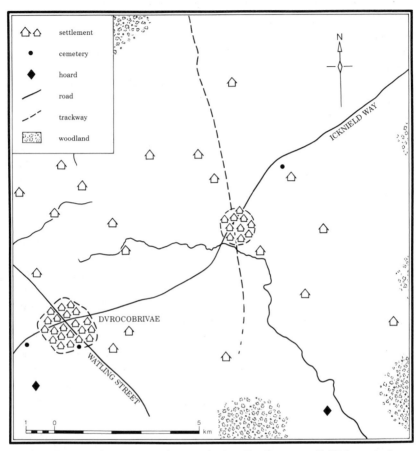

*Settlement of the Luton district during the Romano–British period.*
*(Drawn by Jo Richards.)*

Norfolk, resulted in the destruction of buildings at Colchester, London and St Albans but the countryside in north Hertfordshire and south Bedfordshire was left relatively unscathed. The Boudican revolt apart, the Romans brought peace to the people of southern England, providing a stable environment in which farming, commerce and industry could operate.

By the 3rd century the number of farmsteads in the Luton district had increased considerably, with sites spaced at 1-2 km. intervals in the countryside east of Dunstable. At Limbury a more substantial settlement became established on the Icknield Way which, in south Bedfordshire at least, was now mostly a metalled road with drainage ditches flanking its sides. A track branched off north and possibly southwards towards Farley Hill in the area between Runfold Avenue and Gooseberry Hill and it was at this point that a number of timber-built rectangular houses was built to form a small settlement. This was essentially a farming community, although blacksmithing and metalworking were also practised. Pottery excavated from the site in advance of the laying out of Runfold Avenue and Wodecroft Road in 1953 included fine tablewares imported from France, other tablewares from the Nene valley and near Oxford, and storage jars, cooking vessels and other kitchenwares from north Bedfordshire, the St Albans area and Much Hadham, near Hertford. Farmsteads elsewhere in Luton during the 2nd-early 4th centuries existed at Farley Hill, Butterfield Green and Winch Hill Farm. With individual households and communities generating their own wealth with which they could purchase goods, the late prehistoric twofold social division of nobility and peasantry became diluted to some extent by the emerging classes of administrators, crafts and tradespeople, merchants and prosperous farmers, although a number of administrators and merchants came from other parts of the Roman Empire. In the major towns some individuals were able to afford the cost of building houses out of stone with mosaic floors, plastered walls and underground heating. In the countryside, the more wealthy farmers also lived in luxury houses known as villas. However, whilst the St Albans district supported at least seven villas within a 10 km. radius of the town, the only villa so far identified in the Luton–Dunstable region is at Totternhoe. If reports made earlier this century are to be believed, possible stone buildings with mosaic floors might have existed at the Farley Hill farmstead and at the Bramingham Road end of the Limbury settlement.

In the 3rd century the Romans began to collect taxes in kind, mainly in the form of the corn tax. There was thus no longer the need to accumulate coinage to pay taxes and it is likely that people began to revert back to bartering for goods. Over the next century, the previously flourishing markets contracted. By the mid-4th century much of England was under threat from raids by tribes in Scotland, Ireland and, from across the North Sea, northern Germany. With the decline in the use of coinage and with the general unrest, large numbers of coins were buried in hoards for safekeeping. A pottery vessel found in 1862 near Luton Hoo, which contained about 1,000 3rd century coins buried sometime after AD270, is an example of such a hoard.

In AD410, Rome itself was attacked by tribes from central and eastern Europe and the Roman army was recalled from Britain. The British had to arrange their own defence against external raids and this, in part, was undertaken with the help of mercenary soldiers from Saxony in north-west Germany.

## The Saxons

Saxon soldiers were first invited to protect Britain from raiders but soon the number of Saxon settlers increased as boatloads of migrants from northern Germany arrived on the east coast of England. One group of Saxons, who might have landed in the area of the Wash and travelled along the Icknield Way, settled near Biscot in the mid-5th century, burying their dead in a cemetery that was discovered in the 1920s when the houses at Argyll Avenue were being constructed. By the early 5th century, the Romano-British settlement at Limbury appears to have been abandoned and the market town at Dunstable had contracted in size with the last burials in the cemetery on the south-west side of the town dating to around AD400. In St Albans, though, there is evidence of alterations being made to some of the houses well into the 5th century, suggesting that town life continued here at the time the first Saxon settlers were arriving in Britain. It is thus possible that St Albans was still the main administrative centre for

*The great square-headed brooch, made of gilt bronze, from the Saxon cemetery at Argyll Avenue, near Biscot.*

regulating the distribution of land to the Saxon settlers in north-west Hertfordshire and south Bedfordshire. At present, no other early Saxon cemeteries are known in the north Chilterns, indicating that in north Luton there was land available for colonisation by a Saxon community.

The Argyll Avenue cemetery is amongst the earliest Saxon cemeteries in England, dating from the early 5th to the late 6th centuries. The cemetery includes a minimum of 41 graves. With the exception of three cremations in pottery urns, the burials were inhumations, most of which were accompanied by weapons or jewellery. Some of the objects buried in the graves, for example various ornate brooches, show that the community included some comparatively wealthy members. It is likely that the settlement where the people buried in the cemetery lived was situated between Biscot and Limbury.

Various documents from the late Saxon period recording the arrival of the Saxons have survived. Of these, the Anglo-Saxon Chronicle was compiled in the late 9th century during the reign of King Alfred and is a record of the legends and events believed to have taken place since the late Romano-British period. The account of the happenings of the 5th and 6th centuries is a list of events passed down by oral tradition. Whilst its accuracy can be questioned, it nonetheless gives an impression of political developments during the early Saxon period. The Chronicle records that the West Saxons fought against the Britons at Biedcanforda in 571 and

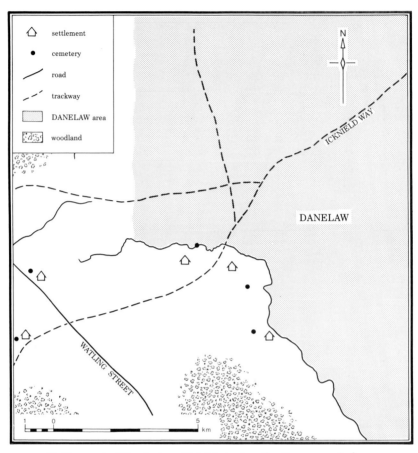

*Settlement of the Luton district during the Saxon period.
(Drawn by Jo Richards.)*

captured the four towns of Lygeanbrig, Aeglesbyrig, Bensingtun and Egonsham. If the site of the battle can be identified as Bedford and, assuming that the towns are listed in the order in which they fell, this suggests an advance along the Icknield Way, with Lygeanbrig being a settlement on the River Lyge or Lea. The settlement of Lygeanbrig could thus have been Limbury, with the cemetery at Argyll Avenue being associated with this settlement.

The late 6th century campaigns led by the West Saxon royal family emanating from Wessex brought the Ouse valley, the Chilterns and the upper Thames valley under their control. At this time, the Argyll Avenue cemetery was extended towards Biscot Mill, where eleven burials were discovered in the 1920s and 1960s. Inhumation burials dating to this period have also been recovered from Dallow Road and immediately south-east of Waulud's Bank, Leagrave. Assuming each of these burial sites is associated with a nearby settlement, this would suggest that there were at least three centres of habitation in Luton during this period at Leagrave, Limbury/Biscot and in the Dallow area. Other farmsteads in the Luton area include Puddlehill, which consisted of a main dwelling house, a bakehouse and a shed for weaving and other craft activities. A small cemetery associated with the farmstead was situated about 200 metres away, the size of which suggests that one family lived there. The hand-made pottery and evidence for weaving, bone working and other craft activities at Puddlehill and other sites of this nature in the Chiltern region indicate that the economic practice established in the Romano-British period of centralised production and trading of pottery and other goods had collapsed and that each community in the early Saxon period was largely self-sufficient.

By the 7th century, society was coalescing into territorial units which, in turn, grouped together to form a network of smaller and greater kingdoms. According to the Tribal Hidage, an 11th-century document with its origins in the 7th or 8th century, the people of south-west Hertfordshire, south Bedfordshire and Buckinghamshire defined themselves as the 'Chilternsoetan'. With other groups in the south-east Midlands, the Chilternsoetan formed the minor kingdom of Middle Anglia, positioned between the greater powers of Mercia to the north west and Anglia to the east. Middle Anglia soon fell under Mercia's control and south Bedfordshire continued to be part of the kingdom of Mercia for the next two centuries. Soon after St Augustus' arrival in Kent in 597 the kingdom of Kent had been converted to Christianity, from where it spread to other kingdoms, with Mercia becoming Christian by the late 7th century. New cemeteries, in some instances alongside pre-7th century cemeteries, were created with graves being orientated east–west, examples of which include Marina Drive, Dunstable and Chamberlain's Barn, Leighton Buzzard. Churches, initially built of wood, were founded for Christian worship at this time, along with the development of the pattern of nucleated villages which is still evident in rural Bedfordshire and much of England today. The position of the church as a centre of local administration began to develop, with King Offa of Mercia giving the land of Biscot to the first Abbot of St Albans in 792, thus continuing the influence of St Albans in the affairs of local residents in the Luton district.

## Danelaw

In the late 8th–9th centuries, Britain was raided on many occasions by the Vikings. By 867, the Vikings had taken control of Northumbria and had started to conquer the other Saxon kingdoms. Their progress was halted in 876, when they were defeated in Wessex by King Alfred. After Alfred had recaptured London in 886, the boundary of land under 'Dane law' was agreed. This ran from London up the River Lea to its source in north Luton, and then in a line to Bedford before heading westwards up the River Ouse to Watling Street. Thus the settlements at Leagrave, Limbury/Biscot and in the Dallow area were on the frontier of the part of England under King Alfred's control, with the land to east of the River Lea being known as Danelaw. The Danelaw was gradually reconquered by Alfred's successors.

## The founding of Luton

Early 10th century written sources refer to a settlement of a few houses surrounding a church at Park Square known as Lygtun or Ligtun: the town on the River Lea. It is possible that this settlement is synonymous with the Saxon settlement in the Dallow area. By 975 Luton was claimed by King Edward the Martyr as a royal town, along with Houghton Regis and

Leighton Buzzard.

At the time of the Norman conquest the Luton district was royal land and, whilst William's armies rampaged northwards from the south coast through Bedfordshire, Luton survived relatively unscathed. When William became king he appointed Ivo Tallebose as sheriff of the manors of Luton and Houghton Regis, who then added Biscot and Sewell to the area under his control. At the time of the Domesday survey commissioned by William in 1086 Luton was the largest Manor in Bedfordshire, stretching from from Streatley to East Hyde.

# THE LOCAL ECONOMY

Luton has been created by the people who have flocked to the town to work in its industries. Many have been attracted to Luton only as a place which combined good wages with affordable housing and it would be interesting, although impossible, to know how many migrants have come to Luton with the firm intention of staying for the rest of their days. Although the industries have changed, it is the people who have taken advantage of the numerous opportunities which the town has presented that have made Luton what it is: a town built upon free trade and private enterprise, working within the parameters of central and local government influence. The pivotal influence in Luton's recent industrial history, however, was marked to a striking degree by conscious co-operation between business and the local authority in a deliberate attempt to alter the town.

## The Early Years

By the time of the Domesday survey in 1086, Luton was a well established town. It had a population of about 700, a market and seven watermills, more than any other manor in the county. The area around the town, about 16,000 acres (6,475 hectares) was a mixture of cultivated land, woodland and waste. The woods were reckoned to be sufficient to support 2,000 pigs. The overall impression given by the survey account is of a prosperous, thriving community.

The mills and the market were important factors in the town's economy, and continued to be so until the end of the

19th century. Luton's historian, William Austin, attempted to locate the sites of the watermills along the River Lea. The first was near the source in Leagrave, and the next at Limbury Mead. These mills had fallen into disuse by the end of the 14th century, but the third mill site continued in use until the middle of the 19th century. This was known as North Mill, and was located near present day Mill Street. It was demolished when the Midland Railway was built. The next one, near the parish church, had disappeared by the 16th century. The fifth

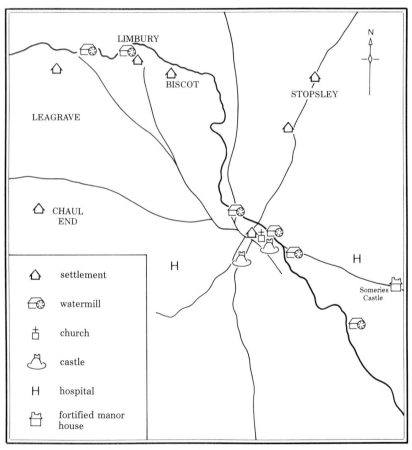

*Luton during the late medieval period. (Drawn by Jo Richards.)*

mill, near present day Osborne Road, was in use until the end of the 19th century; it was known as the Brache Mill. The sixth one, Stapleford Mill, was absorbed into the Luton Hoo estate; it was probably demolished in the 18th century when the Earl of Bute made various improvement to the park. The seventh mill at East Hyde is the only one of the Domesday mills to survive into the 20th century.

Six of the mills belonged to the King, and one to the Church; they were an important source of revenue, since the local people had to have their corn ground there. The river and the mill pond were also a significant source of food supply, particularly for eels and freshwater fish.

Revenue was also collected from the tolls taken at the market, which was held weekly, in the vicinity of the Church. Until about 1200 it was held on Sundays but was then changed to Monday, which is still Luton's official market day. The market was very like open air markets today, with simple stalls made of trestles with boards on top. Local people would come to buy and sell their surplus produce and the town's craftspeople would display their wares for sale. Trade was usually confined to market day, for, in common with most other towns during the medieval period, Luton's retail trade depended upon a collection of craftspeople rather than shopkeepers.

At some time in the 16th century the market was moved to Market Hill; the Market House was built in the middle of the following century, and survived until 1867. In the 16th and 17th centuries Market Hill was sometimes known as Chipping or Cheeping Hill. Many writers in the 18th century commented upon the excellence of Luton's market, particularly the fine quality of the barley that was sold there. These remarks are largely based on statements made in the 16th century that the southern part of Bedfordshire produced 'full, white and big barley' (William Camden) and that Luton was 'a very good market town for barley' (John Leland).

Trading standards at the market were strictly enforced; retail dealing, especially of food, was distrusted as a kind of profiteering and the authorities were quick to invoke the price control regulations. In 1528 John Chamber was fined 2d (1 pence) for selling fish above the market price; at the same court four butchers were fined 8d each for selling meat at too high a price and two innkeepers were fined for making too much profit. In 1535 John Crawley was fined for buying sheep and selling them for a higher price at the same market; this offence, known as regrating, was a common one. In 1546 a directive was issued stating that no one should put hogs or ducks in the market near where grain was sold.

Forestalling was another common offence; market hours were controlled in the buyers' interests so that every one should have an equal opportunity to buy whatever goods were available in the market; in times of scarcity such as after a bad harvest or at the end of winter when food supplies were low the town's authorities were concerned that all should have a fair chance to buy. By controlling the hours of the market it was possible to oversee the transactions to prevent profiteering. As late as 1802 straw hat manufacturers attending the Monday market drew up a list of resolutions; these included agreeing not to buy at the market before the market bell had been rung, and to discontinue the practice of riding about the country to buy plait, which was another method of forestalling the market. The manufacturers believed that by doing this they were 'promoting the real interest of the trade' which was more 'conducive to the benefit of the labourer' as well as being 'to the advantage of the commercial dealer.'

Fairs were much larger occasions than the weekly market; traders would come from London and other large towns with goods that were not easily obtainable in the immediate area. Horses and livestock were bought and sold; entertainment, food and drink would be available and enjoyed. As in many other towns, Luton's fair was held on the day of a church festival, in this case the feast of the Assumption (August 15th); this meant that the entire population of the town, its hamlets and even people from other nearby towns and villages would be free to attend. The fair would start on the evening of the 14th August and continue for up to a week.

Luton's fair was important enough to be the subject of a

dispute between the lord of the manor and the powerful abbey of St. Albans. It was agreed that the rights to the fair were the Abbot's except for the sale of gold, horses, tanned hides and 'of men who of old were sold'. The town's status as a centre for trade was certainly growing, for an archdeacon at Dunstable arbitrating in a case concerning tithes in 1221 cited Luton as a place whose customs could be used as an example to be followed.

The source of the town's wealth and its economic base was agriculture. The majority of people worked on the land, growing enough to support themselves and their families; some also had to work for the lord of the manor as well as cultivating their own small piece of ground, while others followed particular crafts, most of which were related to agriculture and its needs. A tax assessment of 1297 gives some glimpses into the life of Luton in the late 13th century. The basis of the tax was a levy on a ninth of the total value of the tax payers stock, crops, household possessions and trade goods. There were exemptions on some types of goods and no one was taxed whose goods were valued at less than 9 shillings (45 pence), so there is very little information available for many inhabitants of the town and its hamlets (which were included in the return). There were tanners, a cooper, a plough maker, butchers, a tailor and a dyer, and seven merchants whose trade is not specified. No one had any household silver, but two had wooden vessels which were liable to tax; none of the houses in the town or hamlets qualified for special notice but the amount of grain produced was about half of the total from the four towns in the county, namely Bedford, Dunstable, Leighton and Luton.

A few years before the 1297 tax, the chronicler Matthew Paris had described Luton as 'a place abounding with parishioners and richly endowed'. There was indeed something of a population explosion at the end of the 13th century, a fact that would have grave consequences in the following century, for a boom period was about to be followed by a slump. Matthew Paris's description was far from applicable to Luton in the 14th century. For throughout England, that century was a period of famine, plague and social unrest; for the ordinary people of Luton there were many years of great distress and misery.

Following a series of bad harvests there was widespread famine in the years around 1315. Starvation and death resulted. Livestock were affected by an epidemic, probably some form of foot and mouth disease; land was left uncultivated and, with a large population to support, there was consequently little food to go round. The records show that there was a decrease in the number of taxpayers, indicating a decline in wealth if not an actual decline in numbers.

In 1336 a great fire devastated the town. The fire spread quickly and most of the houses, simple constructions of wood and thatch, were soon destroyed. Hundreds of families were made homeless, their barns, stock, tools and equipment ruined. The destruction was so great that the King's tax collectors were ordered to exempt Lutonians until Michaelmas. The number of tax payers in the town had already declined and the combined effects of famine and fire reduced the town considerably. Four years later it was reckoned that 200 houses were vacant in the town and over 700 acres (280 hectares) of land were left uncultivated.

The effects of the fire were exacerbated a few years later in 1349 when the Black Death struck Luton. Having swept through Europe in 1347 the plague reached England in the late summer of the following year. It worked its way across the country, devastating a population already weakened by years of poor harvests and severe winters. Its effects were worse in the towns where people lived in close proximity to one another. Luton was no exception. It is difficult to estimate how many people died in the epidemic but a conservative assessment would be one third to one half of the town's population (approximately 2,000 including the hamlets).

The economic and social changes brought about by the devastation of the first half of the 14th century were profound and far reaching. Population levels had fallen dramatically; labour was scarce and therefore costly, demand outrunning

43

supply. More land was available than there were people to work it, though this did provide an opportunity for some people to rise in society, to consolidate and enlarge their estates.

In the 15th century many landowners in the southern part of Bedfordshire, and certainly in the Luton area, turned to sheep farming since it required less labour than arable farming. This did little to help those at the lower levels of society. At a time when many became richer, many others also became poorer.

Sheep or, more properly, their wool represented wealth and how important they were in the late 15th and early 16th centuries can be seen in the documents of the period. Many instances are recorded in Luton of farmers keeping more sheep than the land could sustain and various attempts were made to remedy this. Sheep are frequently found as bequests in wills: John Sylam of Bramingham left 750 sheep, Valentine Lawrence of Luton left each of his children 20 sheep and £5.00 (a considerable sum in 1500) as well as a sheep to each godchild, and Alice Tychmarsh of Luton left her daughter Joan various household utensils, 10 sheep, 4 cows, and 20 quarters of barley.

Barley was a particularly important crop in the Luton area. Before the expansion of the hat industry in the early 19th century, the town's economic base was agriculture. Even its one major industry, malting, was dependent on the availability of a good supply of locally grown barley. Malting is an essential process in the brewing of beer. Barley is soaked, allowed to germinate and is then roasted in a kiln to provide the raw material for brewing. Ordinary, weak beer was the staple drink for everyone when water was frequently impure and its supply uncertain. Work in the maltings was hard, back breaking; the soaked grain had to be turned regularly to aerate it and, since sprouting grain is no respecter of hours, the maltsters working time was irregular. However, the malting season, autumn through to the spring, was complementary to the agricultural season.

Most of the trade in barley and malt was centred in the

counties of Hertford, Cambridge, Huntingdon and Bedford, where soil conditions, climate and navigable rivers made an ideal combination for barley growing and malt production. The wealth of the brewers, maltsters and barley farmers was remarkable, no more so than in Luton. Malting was well established in the town by the 15th century; it has been estimated that it had over 60 malt kilns at that time. Whatever the precise figure malting, combined with agriculture and its service crafts, was the main occupation of the majority of the townspeople. Some of the Luton maltsters in the 16th century were wealthy men, able to leave considerable sums of money to their heirs, as well as sacks of malt to the poor.

In the late 15th and early 16th centuries some of these wealthy maltsters were members of the Guild of the Holy Trinity. The Guild had been founded in 1474 'for the intent that there should be two chaplains to sing daily within the parish church.' There were many such religious guilds in the country formed to employ priests to say masses for the souls of their members, both living and dead, to relieve the poor, to help members who were in financial or other difficulty. Some guilds, though not Luton's, provided funds to maintain a school. Many also held an annual procession and feast.

The Luton Guild's feast was held towards the end of May. Seldom costing less than £20, and often more, the event was one of lavish feasting and entertainment. In its early years the feast was held in the open but later it moved into the great hall of the Brotherhood House on the corner of Castle Street and Market Hill. Preparations for the feast must have begun some weeks before the event. Food was ordered, ale brewed, staff recruited, equipment hired or made, fuel (wood and charcoal) for cooking obtained, and entertainers engaged. From the Guild's accounts it is possible to estimate the numbers attending the feast and it would appear to be around 200 people. Nearly all the people involved in preparing, supplying and servicing the feast were members of the Guild or closely connected to it. It must have been a major event in Luton's calendar and would have made a considerable impact on the small community of the town at that time.

The Guild was dissolved in 1547 but the turbulent years of the mid 16th century did not effect the economic life of Luton so much as they did other towns in the area such as Dunstable and St.Albans, with their great monastic houses. The parish church was neglected, since no one was sure who was responsible for carrying out repairs. 'At Luton I saw a fair church but the choir roofless, and overgrown with weeds' (Camden's *Britannia*, 1610 translation; first published 1586). Otherwise, the town continued as a prosperous market town, its trades and crafts thriving.

One of the trades growing in importance in 16th and 17th century Luton was brickmaking. Someries Castle, a fortified manor house on the outskirts of Luton, is one of the oldest surviving brick buildings in the country dating from about 1448. The bricks were probably made on site but it is not until the following century that there is evidence of brickmaking in Luton itself. Barnard Spayne was manufacturing bricks and tiles on quite a large scale, possibly in the vicinity of present day Reginald Street/Frederick Street, when he was forcibly ejected from the site and 200 loads of clay removed, because the Lord of the Manor at the time, Sir Thomas Rotheram, claimed that he had extraction rights over the clay as a mineral.

From the time of this incident onwards there is ample evidence to suggest that brickmaking was an established and important industry in the town. In the 18th century John Chalkley, Anthony Sherlock, who was also an innkeeper, Thomas Procter, who came to Luton from Yorkshire, Charles Butcher and Thomas Wood were all working as brickmakers in the town. As the old wattle and daub infilling of timber-framed houses was replaced by brick infill and new buildings were erected, their skills were much in demand. The bricks they made were probably similar to those Luton greys which were to give the town's buildings their characteristic appearance in later years. The purple colour of the bricks is due to the high levels of iron oxide in the brick earth, and the silver grey tone is produced by lime.

In addition to brickmaking and malting, many other crafts

were practised in and around the town. There were the basic
ones which existed in almost every community, large or small,
throughout the country: blacksmiths, carpenters and
wheelwrights were important members of society. There were
craftspeople and merchants in the clothing trades: weavers,
tailors, glovers, drapers; there were also millers, butchers,
bakers and innkeepers. These, however, were the minority;
most people worked in agriculture. This provided the main
source of income, often supplemented by other forms of work;
agricultural labouring in the spring and summer could be
combined with work in the maltings during the winter.

Regular full time employment in one job was an exception
for most people, who made up their income from a variety of
sources. In the 17th and 18th centuries, one additional source
of employment, especially for women, was straw plaiting, for
the embryo hat industry.

An account of the development of Luton's trade and
industry since the end of the Napoleonic Wars can be divided
into three distinct sections, each covering consecutive eras.
The first, lasting for the first three-quarters of the 19th
century, was dominated by the small workshop world of the
straw hat trade. The second, lasting to the end of World War
One, saw both the hat trade at its zenith with an increasing
concentration of production in larger factories and also the
arrival of new engineering industries. The third saw the
expansion of these new firms and the growth of one in
particular, Vauxhall Motors, until it came to dominate all
aspects of local life. With the reduction in the total numbers
employed at Vauxhall from the mid 1970s onwards it is
arguable that Luton is entering a fourth phase of economic
development, although the precise nature and prospects of
success are still uncertain.

## The Hat Industry

Much has been written on the Luton straw hat industry (see
bibliography) and the purpose of this chapter is not to retread
well trod ground but to concentrate upon its effect upon the

lives of local people. The origin of the straw hat industry in this country is unknown, but there is no doubt that by the end of the 17th century it was centred on the east Chilterns area. Its extent can be seen from petitions that were presented to Parliament in 1689 and 1719. The first petition came from the inhabitants of Luton, Dunstable, Studham, Whipsnade, Caddington, Kensworth, Edlesborough, Great Gaddesden, Wingfield, Redbourn, Flamstead, Sundon, Totternhoe and Houghton Regis. The petitioners claimed that 14,000 persons had no other way to support themselves than by making straw hats.

In 1719 a whole series of petitions from the towns and villages of the area were sent to Parliament protesting against the importation of chip plait (plait made from wood shavings) from Holland and straw hats from Italy. The petition from Luton and its hamlets (Stopsley, Leagrave, Limbury, East and West Hyde) was presented on February 3rd 1719. All the petitions stress that it is the poor and 'meaner sort of people' who are most affected by the imports, since the making of straw hats and 'other useful things made of straw' was their sole means of support; without this industry they would be reduced to 'Poverty and Want and become chargeable to the several parishes to which they belong.'

During the 18th century straw plaiting and the making of straw hats was recommended as an employment for the poor and for those who lived in workhouses. In 1724 in Luton's House of Maintenance for the Poor a woman instructed the inmates in plaiting and hat making: 'Their being very old and infirm, or very young and helpless, you must think, little is to be expected from their labour, where nursing is the chief business of the house: and yet there are few of them, but what do bend their hands to the little employment they are put to, which is plaiting of wheat straws; this being a very fine country for the product of that grain, affords a very beautiful straw, which is therefore pitch'd upon as the properest manufacture to employ the poor in; and the farmers are thereby encouraged to draw the finest straws, and cut off the beards before the wheat is threshed, which they make up into bundles as large

*The only photographs of Luton's open air Plait Market were taken on the last time it used George Street before moving to the Plait Halls. Many of the trestles along the length of the street were open to the elements. In fine weather the market presented a colourful, bustling and noisy spectacle but when it rained plait sellers were forced to scuttle for cover wherever they could find it.*

as a wheatsheaf, and sell to the house for 4d. a bundle. A very skilful woman, who is dependent upon the parish, instructs the rest to do their work well, and make no waste. Of the worst work they make ordinary hats and bonnets, and of the best work, they make very good hats, which may be sold there for 3 shillings (15 pence) a piece, but at London would be worth near double the money: and with good management, out of one bundle, 3 hats may be made.'

18th century travellers often made note of the growth of the straw trade. Daniel Defoe (*A Tour through the Whole Island of Great Britain*, 1724) described the manufacture of straw work as having 'greatly increased within a few years past.' In 1746 it was reported that 'about Dunstable and Luton they make straw hats and other things of that sort, which manufactures find business for several thousand people.' (*The Agreeable Historian*). Later in the century the number of references to the industry increase; Nathaniel Spencer, for example, in his *'Complete English Traveller'*, 1772, describes Luton as 'a handsome town, situated between two hills, and the inhabitants carry on a considerable manufactory of straw hats.'

Both the plaiting and sewing of straw into hats were cottage industries, particularly in Luton, but from the early 19th century plaiting became increasingly confined to the rural areas with the better paid sewing to be found in the towns. By the middle of the century a straw plaiter could earn between four and six shillings (20 to 30 pence) a week in an occupation which not only absorbed females but also men and boys as a secondary source of income. Because the cost of the plait accounted for a fifth of the finished selling price plaiters had to work continuously in order to earn an average amount a week and few plaiters could afford to travel to a plait market where the best price for their wares could be obtained and instead sold on to a plait dealer who travelled around the villages, or to the local grocer, occasionally in return for goods, and from whom the least price could be obtained. The reduction in import duties from 1842 opened up this poorest paid branch of the hat industry to foreign competition through imported plait from Italy and Switzerland, and then to cheap imports from the far east which finally killed it.

Although hat sewing was undertaken in the villages it was concentrated in the towns where the sewer, like the plaiter, was paid by the piece. In a large hat factory (employing between 100–500 persons) a swift, experienced sewer could earn approximately 18 shillings (90 pence) a week and in smaller establishments anything between 8–15 shillings (40–75 pence) a week. These earnings for women can be compared with those of men where a bleacher or dyer in a hat factory could earn between 12–15 shillings (60–75 pence) a week and an agricultural labourer around 8 shillings (40 pence) a week.

*E.B. Thompson, a plait merchant, photographed in 1908 at the Cheapside Plait Halls. Some plait dealers were specialists but, particularly in the early stages of the trade, many were also shopkeepers and publicans.*

Sewing straw hats was an attractive proposition for most young girls in the south-east midlands when compared with the poor pay and drudgery of the alternatives – plaiting, lacemaking, farmwork, domestic service or early marriage. Thousands of girls would migrate into Luton during the busiest of periods of hat making (usually between December and May) from the surrounding towns and villages in Bedfordshire, Buckinghamshire and Hertfordshire for the relatively high wages which could be earned: New Town in 1841 contained nearly three times as many women as men in the age brackets between eleven and thirty.

Because it was not significantly mechanised (sewing machines did not begin to become widespread until the 1870s and blocking machines also were not developed until the middle of the century) the hat industry did not require heavy capital investment and it was relatively easy to set up in business. It was, however, heavily dependent upon export and fashion and as such could be a precarious industry also.

*Gray and Horn's stall in the Plait Halls.*

Flexibility and adaptability was of great importance in all aspects of the industry and this crucial element is most evident in Luton. Until the onset of widespread mechanisation in the latter years of the 19th century only a small proportion of the local manufacture of hats took place entirely within the large factories in the centre of town. An estimated three-quarters of the work was undertaken in small production units based in Luton's houses to which various stages of work, usually sewing, was farmed out as demand dictated. Land was plentiful and therefore within range of the investor of modest means.

Mechanisation did not mean the end of the small makers, for it was possible to hire sewing machines for half a crown (12.5 pence) a week, so enabling them to compete with the larger manufacturers. However, many of the makers lived not far from the edge of poverty especially during the slack season.

The trade was open to abuse and exploitation; bankruptcy and failure were common – one street in the town was known as Rotten Row. Despite this they continued to work, preferring their independence and high earnings in the busy season to

*A hat sewing room in an unidentified Luton factory c.1907.*

working for someone else.

Although straw plaiting had declined steeply by the end of the 19th century (disappearing altogether by the 1930s), the hat industry flourished and thrived on imported plaits and mechanisation. An added impetus was given by the introduction of felt hat making in the early 20th century. To a large extent this overcame the seasonality of the industry, and it was helped along by the beginnings of the millinery trade. While the important role of the straw machinist declined, more work was provided for women in the designing and trimming of hats.

*Asher Hucklesby's hat factory in George Street with Bond Street, his own road, running alongside. Hucklesby's was one of a number of hat factories which had dominated George Street's landscape since the 1850s.*

During World War One the hat industry contracted and changed; it lost many of its export markets, albeit temporarily. In the inter-war period its adaptability came to the fore as the trade came to terms with rapidly changing circumstances. The use of straw plait decreased – supplies were seriously affected by the war between China and Japan – but there was an increasing use of imported 'exotics', such as sisal and hemp as well a considerable expansion of the felt hat production. By 1939 the making of women's felt hats accounted for three quarters of the trade but by this time engineering had overtaken the hat industry as the town's main employer, altering its industrial structure; 35.5% of workers were now engaged in engineering, while 24% worked in the hat trade. World War Two also brought about many changes. The trade, already considerably reduced from its peak at the end of the 19th century, was diminished even further by the closure of many of the smaller firms. At one stage there was even a threat to transfer the entire industry elsewhere; the town's response was immediate, for as one councillor said at the time such a removal would 'tear the heart out of Luton'. There was a feeling of relief when the proposal was dropped.

The devastation of the London hat-making area during the war brought a number of new companies to the town, but as the fashion for wearing hats has declined, so has their manufacture. Although very far from being the staple of the town's industry, it is still a feature of its economy, and continues to exhibit its characteristics of flexibility and adaptability as new materials are employed to make headwear of every shape and variety imaginable.

## 19th Century Luton: Other Trades

Although the straw hat trade provided Luton with a distinctive staple trade, it dovetailed and co-existed with other industries requiring predominantly male labour complementing hat manufacture with its overwhelming preponderance of women. Luton ceased to be a market town and consequently the economic function of the seasonal fairs also declined. The Fox Fair, held in the vicinity of the present Telford Way, disappeared in the early 19th century and the annual Statute Fair, or 'Stattie', held in late summer and at which labourers would hire themselves out for the coming year became an anachronism: by the late 1850s just a handful boys were on hand for hire and the fair was abolished in 1880. The name 'Stattie' was subsequently transferred to the annual April Fair which continued still selling livestock until the Borough Council closed it in 1929. Agriculture was a dwindling component of the local economy but in 1900 there were still eight farms within a mile radius of the Town Hall and three times that number a little further beyond.

Brewing continued to provide a significant undercurrent to Luton's economic life with the leading brewers being amongst

*J. W. Green stands proudly outside his brewery in Park Street West. By 1900 Green possessed a brewing empire of more than 150 tied houses.*

the most important men in the town, a position maintained by the absorption of the smaller concerns into larger businesses. In the first half of the 19th century the biggest was owned by the Burr family whose brewery was on Park Square. The Burr's sold out to Thomas Sworder, who already owned the Crown and Anchor brewery in Manchester Street, in 1857. Sworder in turn sold his brewery and 90 or so tied houses 40 years later to J. W. Green, who had been steadily building up his small brewing empire through the acquisition of smaller concerns, including that of Pearmans, on Market Hill: upon the death of Daniel Pearman in 1857 his two sons, who were far more interested in enjoying money than making it, rapidly ran the business into trouble, making it easy prey for Green. By 1900 he owned the largest brewing business in the district, numerous public houses in south Bedfordshire and north

Hertfordshire, and an elegant villa, Rookwood, along the New Bedford Road. He still persisted however, in saving the nearly spent remnants of the bars of soap from his bathroom, soaking the various fragments together in order to make up another bar and thus save himself unnecessary expense.

The inexorable spread of Luton's streets from the 1830s onwards also provided employment of various kinds in the land market and building industry. Timber merchants, surveyors, bricklayers, decorators, building society clerks, labourers and landlords: there were numerous opportunities presenting themselves in a town growing on the back of the straw hat trade. From the viewpoint of the county town an astonished *Bedfordshire Times* commented: 'for some years past everyman who could scrape a few pounds together has built himself a house; success has encouraged him to further speculations, and cases have occurred of labourers and

*A brickpit at Round Green in 1909, one of seven which at various times existed in the Stopsley district. Standing in the pit is the Dunstable-based antiquarian, Worthington G. Smith, for whom the brickpits were convenient excavations providing him with much information about the locality before the last glaciation.*

journeymen mechanics erecting whole streets'. This was a bit of an exaggeration but it does indicate the sort of town which Luton had become, although there were no large scale quick killings to be made and there were no vast concerns, even the biggest building firms such as Smith's or Williams' probably employing no more than 20 or so men. A large number of builders operated on the verge of insolvency and some, for example William Attwood, went out of business only to start up again.

Many Lutonians drew upon a variety of incomes, an approach which gave a measure of greater security when so much in the town depended upon the fickle fortunes of the hat trade. For example, a beershop keeper in New Town could also use his premises as a base for buying and selling straw plait, he could be the landlord of a handful of cottages in the district, and in the busy season let out rooms in his beershop as lodgings for hat sewers. A real and loftier example is F. C. Scargill, who owned Bramingham Shott (now Wardown Park) and pursued a legal career with a practice in King Street, also serving as Clerk to the Justices; in addition he owned a local newspaper, a handful of beershops, Biscot Mill and lent money for mortgages. Luton was not an attractive town, but it was a place of opportunity, drawing in thousands of hopeful people from the surrounding region. The sum total of all their enterprise, ambition, graft, exploitation, profiteering, speculation, failure and success, for better or for worse, laid the foundations of the modern town.

## The New Industries

Agriculture, brewing and housing were important sub-components of the local economy but in the minds of a number of Luton's leading citizens, the town was still too dependent upon its main industry. When Luton became a borough in 1876 the men who ran the town's businesses now found themselves responsible for the future of the place that they had helped to make. Developments in the years between 1895 and 1910 were subsequently to transform the town and this is a period which still requires extensive research, although the data available might not answer all the questions which are posed. What should be remembered is that Luton at this time was still a small town and that the men who ran the town's industries and were members of the Chamber of Commerce, also sat together on the Town Council, were members of the same local Liberal Party (which dominated local politics), were often affiliated to the same religious denomination and were the same men behind the various syndicates which were speculating upon land. In such a small town these men were frequently related through marriage. This is not to present a picture of a conspiratorial caste, stitching up the future of Luton in smoke-filled rooms; membership of the above bodies was fluid, with some men being attached to just one or two groupings. It serves, however, to point out that in a small, relatively compact town like Luton, there were numerous short cuts to decision making.

*William Bigg, arguably the most influential Lutonian of the 19th century. He provided the moral guidance, business acumen and financial prop in a variety of spheres including the Board of Health, Water Company, Gas Company, railways, libraries, education, local politics and the Chamber of Commerce, which was established at his instigation. He was a keen walker and it was on one of his strolls that he chose his burial plot in a quiet, unobtrusive corner of the General Cemetery.*

William Bigg, a Quaker, promoter of education, backer of the Luton Water Company, bank manager and the first Mayor of Luton in 1876, had created a local branch of the Chamber of Commerce as one of his first actions upon becoming Mayor. From the Council and the Chamber came the New Industries

59

Committee in 1889, formed in a deliberate attempt to diversify the town's economic base by attracting firms other than hat factories to the town. By the end of the 1890s Luton was promoting its virtues to the commercial sector at large. Principally at the behest of the Secretary to the Chamber of Commerce, Thomas (later Sir Thomas) Keens, a publicity booklet entitled 'Luton as an Industrial Centre' was published outlining the reasons why new firms should wish to move to Luton. Amongst Luton's proclaimed virtues was cheap electricity, thanks to the Corporation-owned Electricity Station built in 1900 (due to the initiative of hat factory manager, councillor and land syndicate member Albert Wilkinson) and low rates. There was no tradition of trade union organisation in the town, a factor which could increase labour costs and there was plenty of affordable land, much of which was close to the railway line which linked Luton with London.

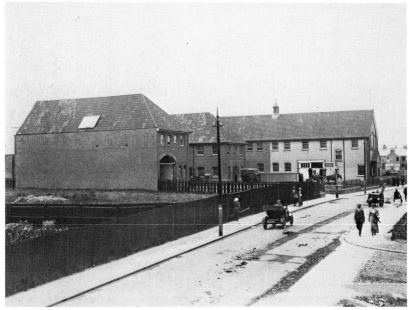

*Commer Cars' factory in Biscot Road shortly after the company arrived in Luton in 1906. The factory was demolished to make way for houses in 1985.*

Two of the principal non-hat firms, Hayward Tyler and Balmforths, were already established adjacent to each of the town's two railway lines when the first of the influx of new firms, Laporte's, relocated to Luton in 1898. They were followed, amongst others, by the CWS Cocoa Works (with its distinctive aroma) in 1902, the British Gelatine Works (1903), Commercial (later Commer) Cars (1906), Davis Gas Stove Company (1907), George Kent's (1908), SKF Ball Bearing Company (1910) and Adamant Engineering (1919). Many of these firms brought employees with them and during their early years in the town they altered and broadened their production range. All influenced Luton to varying degrees but one above all others was to dramatically alter the town, replacing dependence upon the hat trade with a dependence upon itself: Vauxhall.

## Vauxhall Motors and Modern Industry

*Casting in Kent's factory during World War One.*

It is engineering, far more than the straw hat trade, which has shaped modern Luton. Arguably, it is Vauxhall Motors which has been more influential in defining the dimension, character and affluence of the town than all the other industrial components put together. For the first 25 years of its existence in Luton there was nothing to indicate that Vauxhall would develop at a significantly greater rate than any other commercial concern: the firm had arrived in 1905 following a merger with the West Hydraulic Company and, with 180 employees, began turning out a varied range of products but principally pumping machinery. The manufacture of motor cars was just a sideline which resulted in the creation of a

*With a shortage of male labour during World War One thousands of women were recruited to the munitions factories which were located on the outskirts of town around Dallow and Chaul End. It was amongst the women of these factories that Luton's first instances of union organisation, and the earliest strike, occurred.*

separate company in 1907 under Leslie Walton and Percy Kinder. For the next few years Vauxhall became noted for producing large cars which featured prominently in rallying events.

The best accounts of Vauxhall's development are those produced by Len Holden (see bibliography). Holden emphasises the failure of the company to anticipate the change in the car market after World War One when the introduction of cheap, mass-produced cars by Ford, Austin and Morris began to squeeze out the medium luxury cars in which firms like Vauxhall specialised. With the company facing the same bleak future which was taking a toll of other small British firms deliverance came about in the form of the American giant General Motors which took over Vauxhall in 1925. During the late 1920s GM began re-organising production methods at Vauxhall toward the more efficient assembly line system and, with heavy investment, steered the company's product range toward the mass market. The Cadet, launched in 1930, was an

*Two years before the official opening of Luton Airport in 1938, an aircraft production company established by Captain Edgar Wickner Percival was started on the site of Eaton Green Farm, adjacent to the developing aerodrome. Pictured here is a Percival Provost at Luton Airport.*

attempt to fill a niche of its own, a fraction higher in quality than its rivals and this was followed by entry into the truck market with a two tonner for the first time carrying the name 'Bedford'.

Vauxhall's revival from the this time owes as much to the personnel which GM installed at the top of the firm as it does to the greater investment which the parent company was able to inject. The running of the company was left to the British board headed from 1930 until 1953 by Charles (later Sir Charles) Bartlett and its twin achievements were not only in steadily increasing Vauxhall's share of the domestic car market but also in transforming the company into virtually a paragon of good industrial relations, a place to work which attracted thousands of people. With much of Britain's older industries suffering from debilitating bouts of depression and recession during the 1920s and 1930s, Luton's new firms expanded: whilst unemployment stood at over 20% nationally in 1932, it was only half that proportion in Luton (11.4%) and the recently established firms were being joined by others, Electrolux and Percival Aircraft being two of the most notable. Luton, therefore, with its new and varied industries presented an enticing combination of secure jobs, good pay and homes. Migrants came to the town from the depressed regions of Britain especially Scotland, the north-east, and south Wales but although these people stood out by virtue of their distinctive accents and social organisation, the bulk of the newcomers to Luton were in fact from London and the south-east of England.

Luton's economy generally presented an attractive haven but Vauxhall in particular was where many people wished to be taken on and the main reason was clear enough: high wages. It was possible to earn anywhere between 30–50% more at Vauxhall than at the bigger engineering and hat firms in the town. Wages were high to attract workers who were needed to man the mass production system but this created a greater demand for jobs than it was possible to satisfy: people waited for years to be taken on at Vauxhall and it was not until the demands of war-time production and conscription to the

*Dr John Dony, 1899–1991. Luton born and bred, John Dony was a botanist, local historian and acknowledged expert of the workings of Luton's hat trade – the subject for which he was awarded a Ph.D in 1941. Dr Dony was Senior Master for History and Economics at Luton Grammar School until his retirement in 1964, Honorary Keeper of Botany at Luton Museum from 1935 until 1988 and was a leading member of many local societies as well as being the author of eleven local books plus numerous articles and leaflets. He became an Honorary Fellow of the Linnean Society of London in 1954 (an award he dearly cherished) and was made an MBE in 1983. Surprisingly, he was never honoured by his home town through being given the Freedom of the Borough, although the natural history Field Centre on the Bushmead estate was named after him upon its completion in 1990. (Reproduced by permission of C. M. Dony.)*

A painting by Carlton Smith depicting the sewing of straw hats. Although few working environments would have been as romantic or leisurely as this, the painting does show that the occupation was clean and also shows the elderly lady to be plaiting straw whilst the younger girls are engaged in the more lucrative work of sewing the hats. When this was painted in the 1890s, straw plaiting was already in sharp decline.

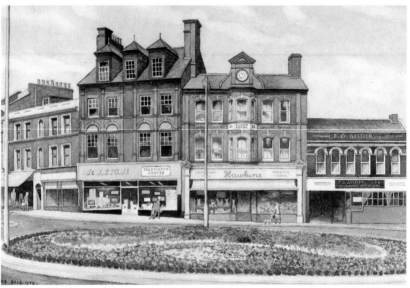

Park Square, painted by James Gale in 1972, shortly before the demolition of these shops to make way for the Arndale Centre.

*The Market Halls painted by Charles Page in 1972.*

*An artist's impression of Luton's market day at the beginning of the*
*Inns abounded on George Street, including the George Hotel, the Bell*
*the Shoulder of Mutton (right). Luton's Market House stands between*

*...ry: this view looks toward Market Hill, also known as Chipping Hill.*
*...s Keys, the Black Swan, the Foot Plough, the Kings Arms (centre) and*
*...two. (Drawn by Jo Richards.)*

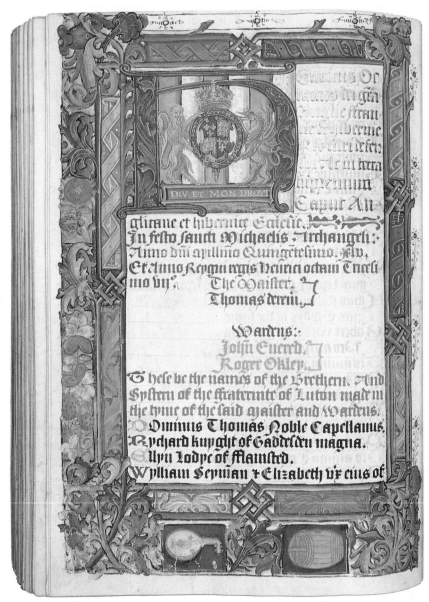

*A page from the register of the Guild of the Holy and Undivided Trinity and the Blessed Holy Mary. Luton's Guild, in common with other fraternities around the country (there were seventeen in Bedfordshire), had a religious, social, economic and political function. The register lists more than 6,000 members and supporters.*

A painting of the Peace Day Riot around midnight on 19-20 July, 1919.
Legend has it that the Town Hall clock struck twelve and then fell out.
Earlier in the evening the Mayor had fled the building dressed in disguise.

A painting by George Shepherd in 1823 entitled 'Old Cottages at Luton'
with St. Mary's visible in the background. The location of this building
is not certain but was possibly on the site of the railway line in front of
Hart Hill. (Private Collection.)

*Luton Girls Choir at the Alma c. 1950.*

*The Hospice at Bramingham, opened in 1991.*
*(Photograph by Chris Grabham.)*

armed forces that the waiting lists were reduced. Holden cites examples of men living in north London who found it worthwhile to cycle to work and back each day until a permanent move to Luton could be arranged.

It would be wrong however, to attribute Vauxhall's success entirely to high wages attracting the numbers of workers required to meet the investment plans of General Motors. Bartlett was a shrewd leader who dispelled the company's

*Charles Bartlett, the popular and highly successful Chairman of Vauxhall Motors from 1930 until 1953*

old regime of arbitrary, despotic and inefficient management and extracted a degree of compliance from the workforce which was the envy of other car companies. Good basic pay was boosted by a productivity related Group Bonus System and a Profit Sharing Scheme. Various sickness benefits, also available to the families of workers, and pension and holiday entitlements further increased the attractiveness of the company. The potential for trouble was curbed by the introduction of the Management Advisory Committee (M.A.C.) in 1941 which comprised representatives of management, foremen and shop floor workers. Management was accessible, even benevolent and Reg (later Sir Reginald) Pearson, Bartlett's deputy and one of a number of senior executives promoted from the shop floor, estimated that he spent up to three quarters of his time on personnel matters. Whereas once membership of a trade union would result in dismissal Bartlett recognised their role within the company but dealt with just two: the A. E. U., representing most of the skilled workers, and the N. U. V. B., later to be absorbed into the T. G. W. U. Bartlett's reforms were eventually dismantled by their own success: the company outgrew the M. A. C. which just could not cope with the far greater number of workers that it was supposed to represent. Following Bartlett's retirement American management began to assume a greater influence, a factor which manifested itself not only in the gradual disappearance of his structures but also in the introduction of scaled-down American-style cars such as the Cresta, the Victor and the Viscount. Much of the close, even harmonious, relationship between management and the workforce also diminished from this time but it was a measure of Bartlett's and Pearson's legacy that rarely did problems become as bitter or as entrenched as at other car companies in the U. K.

Vauxhall built a formidable array of sporting and social

*The Vauxhall Spectacular in 1972.*

clubs and their annual Vauxhall Spectacular drew thousands of Lutonians to the Brache. When General Motors took over the company its workforce totalled just under 2,000. By 1950 this figure stood at 12,659 and by the 1960s the numbers employed at the Luton and Dunstable plants making cars and Bedford trucks were twice this figure: this was five times as many as SKF, the next biggest employer in the town. Many more depended indirectly upon Vauxhall for their livelihood and, despite the warnings of the *Luton News* and Bartlett himself, Luton had become as dependent upon this one company as it had been upon the hat trade a century earlier. Much to the chagrin of their employers, workers at other factories in Luton demanded levels of pay and other benefits which approached those at Vauxhall and when, in 1946, the main employer started shutting its factory for two weeks every

*FB Victors and HA Vivas move down the line in the Paint Shop at Vauxhall during the late 1950s. (Photograph courtesy of Vauxhall Motors.)*

*An aerial photograph showing the extent of the Vauxhall Motors factory in the 1950s. Already at this time Luton was being called 'a small town just outside Vauxhall'.*

summer, so much else in the town closed up also that other employers were forced to follow suit and grant this period of leave to its own workforce. Even the local education authority had to fall into line with the Vauxhall fortnight and adjust the commencement of its school holidays accordingly.

Luton thus had found its recent industrial history repeating itself: no-one connected with the New Industries Committee could have foreseen what the results of their work would be, although the amount of land purchased by the syndicates indicates that some at least appreciated the extent to which the town would develop. The future is also hard to predict but there are some pointers. Vauxhall Motors steadily increased their share of the motor car market in the 1980s through automation and the separation of trucks, vans and cars with the creation of the short-lived AWD Ltd. and IBC where work practises owe more to Japanese than

*SKF's factory at Leagrave Road in 1944. A second site at Sundon Park had been established two years earlier.*

Anglo-American methods. With the development of the successful Nova–Astra–Cavalier range Vauxhall, with a 16.1 % share in the market in 1991, is now a serious rival to Ford (U.K.) for the position of leading car producer in Britain and productivity has risen dramatically. This has not, however, been carried out with a still further increase in its presence in Luton. The workforce has instead contracted to 6,500 at Vauxhall's Luton plants and 2,200 at IBC (1991) as GM has taken advantage of its European-wide assembly and manufacturing capabilities. With the extent of the company's long-term commitment to the town uncertain, Luton has so far failed to diversify sufficiently to make up for the gap being left not only by Vauxhall but also by the other large employers in the town which have contracted either their operations or workforce or both. The number of people employed in the service sector grew to the point that by 1989 it contained almost twice as many Luton people as in manufacturing (61% and 32.2% respectively) and there is no sign of that trend being reversed. Ominously, the development at Capability Green has realised to date barely half its hoped for take up. In the spring of 1992 unemployment in Luton climbed to more than 11% of the workforce: this was 2% higher than the national average, 2.75% higher than the average for south-east England as a whole and 3% higher than the county average. These figures do not tell the full story, as improved communications allow people to commute to work in Luton without having to live there but it is still clear that the town's reputation as an employment haven is no longer applicable. As Luton entered the 20th century it was a town which was able to provide the framework for successful industrial expansion through local control of commercial rates and the supply of land, electricity, water and gas. Circumstances are very different now: at the end of *The Story of Luton*, Dyer and Dony concluded 'the town never stood still and what the future holds for it will be largely its own making'. Wherever decisive influence over Luton's future lies, be it Whitehall, the United States, Europe or Japan, one suspects that its destiny is not at present in its own hands.

| Population of Luton | | | |
|---|---|---|---|
| *Census* | *Population* | *Census* | *Population* |
| 1821 | 2,986 | 1901 | 36,404 |
| 1831 | 3,961 | 1911 | 49,978 |
| 1841 | 5,827 | 1921 | 61,342 |
| 1851 | 10,648 | 1931 | 70,486 |
| 1861 | 15,329 | 1951 | 110,381 |
| 1871 | 17,317 | 1961 | 131,505 |
| 1881 | 23,960 | 1971 | 161,178 |
| 1891 | 30,053 | 1981 | 163,209 |
|  |  | 1991 | 171,671 |

# THE PHYSICAL GROWTH OF THE TOWN

Accurate information about population figures before the introduction of the official census is very difficult to obtain; all figures before 1801 are approximations. At the time of the Domesday survey in 1086, Luton's population was estimated to be about 700. By the late 13th century this had risen to about 2,000, although this figure includes the hamlets of Leagrave, Limbury, Stopsley, East and West Hyde; about half that figure would have lived in the township itself.

The town was centred around the parish church, which provided a focus for many activities such as the market and courts. The church was located at the crossing point of the ways leading out of the town – towards Hitchin, St. Albans and, via the future George Street, Bedford and Dunstable. Most of the town's houses and cottages were located in this area.

Very little is known about the homes of the ordinary people of Luton during the medieval period, but they were probably like most other houses and cottages of the time: simple timber-framed constructions with walls of wattle and daub and thatched roofs. The majority would have consisted of one main room, the hall, with a central hearth; all household activities, cooking, eating and sleeping took place in this one space. A bench or form would provide seating, and beds were usually straw palletts laid on the floor; cooking equipment consisted of a large pot suspended over the fire, with wooden bowls and spoons for eating. The more affluent would have had an additional room or chamber for sleeping and private use.

The devastations of the 14th century depleted Luton's population considerably and it took a very long while for the

71

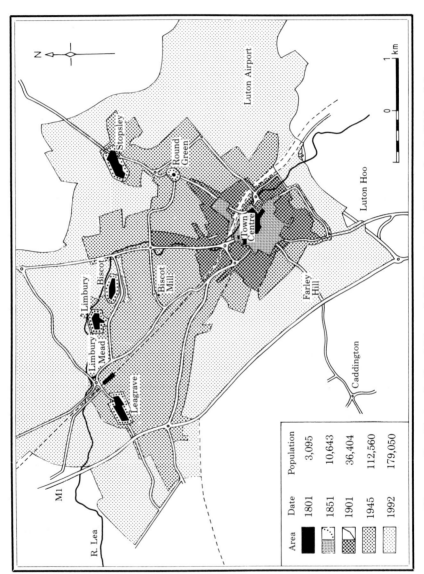

The growth of Luton in the 19th and 20th centuries. (drawn by Jo Richards).

| Area | Date | Population |
|---|---|---|
| | 1801 | 3,095 |
| | 1851 | 10,643 |
| | 1901 | 36,404 |
| | 1945 | 112,560 |
| | 1992 | 179,050 |

town to recover anything like its previous size and importance. By the 16th century the population of the town and its hamlets had reached about 1,500; by the end of the 17th century, 200 hundred years later, the figure had increased to about 2,000. This slow rate of growth is a reflection of national statistics, for in 1600 the country as a whole had fewer inhabitants than it had had in 1300.

In the early 17th century, the town seems to have had a housing problem. It is difficult to ascertain the precise nature of this, but it would seem that there was a shortage of low cost accommodation, houses or cottages, for the town's poorer inhabitants, or that those who were better off were suffering a period of recession and were seeking to maximise their assets and to avoid paying the rates which were levied as part of the Poor Law system introduced at the end of the 16th century. In 1618 Sir Robert Napier and Francis Crawley wrote to the Privy Council expressing their concern: 'For the town of Luton being a good market town having many fair dwelling houses fronting to the street, most whereof have large malthouses, and other necessary houses belonging to them, was inhabited by men of good estate, who practising the trade of malting, both enriched themselves, set a work many poor people, and were well able and did give relief to the many poor inhabitants there. But may it please your Lordships now of late some respecting only their private gain (although with the ruin of the whole town) do pull down, and sell away the fairer part of those houses, and make several cottages of the rest. To which they admit poor tenants that have no certain livelihood, but are likely in a short time they and their children to overgrow and oppress the whole parish.' The document then goes on to list the buildings and their owners but the success or otherwise of the petition is not known.

Until the early 19th century the town changed remarkably little in its physical spread. Park Street, George Street and Church Street were the main thoroughfares, with narrow lanes and ways leading from them. The thatched, timber-framed houses were slowly replaced by brick and tile buildings, or were improved by the addition of a facade. Chimneys had started to be used by the 16th century, as had the use of glass in windows.

By the 16th century there were other signs of affluence inside the house, especially in the homes of those who were better off such as craftspeople, merchants and yeoman farmers, with furniture, textiles and a wide range of household utensils to improve their standard of living. For example, Jelyan Kylbye, who died in 1546, had two painted coffers in her house as well as painted hangings on the wall; a few years later, Joan Chalkeley, a widow, had a long table, 8 stools, 4 chairs, 2 spinning wheels, books, pewter and brass implements as well as bed and table linen. However, these are the people, prosperous, fortunate citizens, who had enough property to make wills and to leave documentary evidence about their material possessions and way of life. For many inhabitants of the town, such as servants and labourers, there is scant information.

By 1800, Luton's population had grown to about 3,000 but the town itself would have been recognisable to a resident from the late medieval period, as for several centuries Luton remained a place of two main streets from which five others, plus a number of lanes and courtyards, also ran. St. Mary's Church remained at the hub of the town and on the site of present day Park Square was Long Pond, stagnant and smelly, especially in summer. George Street contained four farms and a row of trees: a large chestnut stood in front of the site of the present Town Hall. All the streets had grass covered banks and the roads, frequently described as 'dirty', were so narrow that it was difficult for two carts to pass one another. The houses were 'low', with overhanging stories and built with either thatched roofs or moss covered tiles and open gutters. The River Lea was far more substantial than today and occasionally burst it banks in heavy rainfall, sometimes with loss of life. The town was flooded in 1795 when one member of the Brown family was washed away and drowned, and again in 1828. Although no-one was killed on the latter occasion several houses were so badly damaged that they required rebuilding. By 1850, the distinctive shape and balance of this homely,

*A remnant of the old market town: Peddars Cottage in Upper George Street, photgraphed on 6th October 1899, shortly before its demolition.*

grubby market town had been obliterated by industrial change and it was the distinctive nature of Luton's industry which gave the town its character and appearance. A marked feature of Luton's growth from the mid-19th century onward was the abundance of relatively cheap building land.

## 19th Century Expansion

The land in the parish of Luton was owned by several families of whom two, the Butes at Luton Hoo and the Crawleys of Stockwood, owned by far the most. Although the Bute lands in the centre encircled the township in an almost unbroken band there were also other families with land holdings in the heart of Luton, the most notable names being those of Gutteridge, Chase, Burr and Waller. The latter three families, like the Butes, had established themselves in Luton during the middle of the 18th century. It is apparent that a considerable amount of purchase and exchange of land took place from this time although, unlike many other parishes in England, Luton never experienced an all encompassing Act of Enclosure which clarified the control and ownership of portions of land and, as a result, evidence for what was going on locally is scanty.

In a period of 25 years from 1831 all the principal landowning families, with the exception of the Crawleys, were eclipsed by death or removal. The key departure was that of the Marquess of Bute who sold the bulk of his Luton Hoo estate in 1844 in order to finance development on his Glamorgan property, namely the Bute docks in Cardiff. Only the lands in the centre of Luton were excluded from the sale, and these were periodically sold off without control or condition when the Bute Trustees deemed it advantageous. With

*Most of Luton's sub-standard housing was swept away in successive clearance programmes during the 1930s. This example at 38, New Town Street, survived until 1956.*

buoyant periods in the hat trade being followed by great demand for building ground, the pressure grew upon the remaining estates to sell up and this was usually done when one of the smaller landowners died or retired and moved away.

Luton initially grew in two areas on the outskirts of the old township: New Town and High Town. These districts immediately became synonomous with constant building and, with no local authority existing to control the standard of building, the two districts soon acquired a high proportion of slum housing to go with some of the older, squalid courtyards in the town centre. Although there were abundant supplies of brick close by, some houses were built of wood or other materials, many possessed tiny rooms with dangerous stairways and a considerable number of the worst contained no amenities for lighting, heating, water supply or sanitation. The establishment of the Board of Health in 1850s curbed the most blatant excesses of unregulated building but was not able

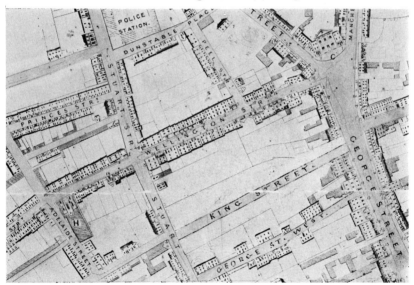

*Wellington Street in 1862. Originally a private road, the lower end of Wellington Street initially contained a high proportion of elegant homes for Luton's small band of professionals, a handful of hat factories and shops, as well as The Eagle public house on the corner with Peel Street. (Reproduced with permission of Bedfordshire Record Office.)*

to remove the slums already in existence and it was not until the 1930s that Luton Borough Council possessed the power, resources and the will to undertake wholesale demolition of substandard housing. By enforcing minimum standards of building the local Board of Health contributed much to Luton's 19th century landscape: rows of solid, comfortable, brick built terraced houses with private yards at the rear. Uniformity was enlivened by varieties of architectural decoration around windows, doorways and eaves. Rapid though Luton's growth had been, outstripping all of its neighbours, it remained a small town. The population of some 10,000 in the mid-19th century had tripled by its end.

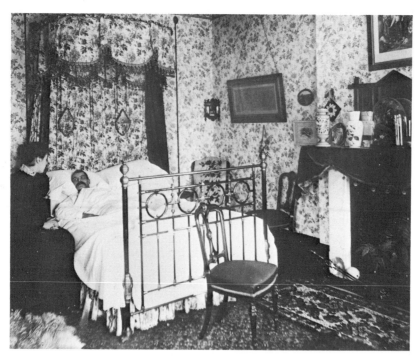

*The interior of a middle class home in 1897.*

## 20th Century Acceleration

By 1900 most of the land once owned by the Marquess of Bute and the other principal estate owners had been sold off. The town broadly comprised three districts, New Town, High Town and Park Town, the latter formerly known as Brown Brick. There were smaller developments in other pockets such as north of the Town Hall between Dunstable Road and New Bedford Road. The proportion of people who owned their own homes, or who had a part share in them, is difficult to calculate but was possibly in the region of between 15% and 20%, a figure significantly higher than the national average. Given the nature of the local economy Luton did not possess a substantial managerial or professional middle-class and as an industrial town it did not attract legions of London commuters or, as in the case of Bedford, retired colonial staff. There was not, therefore, sufficient demand to produce distinctive middle class suburbs apart from the tiny enclave on Hart Hill or the half a mile stretch of small villas along the New Bedford Road. Instead, there was a remarkable degree of intermixing with, for example, the elegant homes of George Street West backing directly upon the notorious slums in Adelaide Terrace described in 1850 as a place where the 'stench is intolerable'.

Much of the building development which took place in the 19th century did so in a piecemeal, unco-ordinated fashion by builders who were small operators seeking to obtain as rapid return as possible for their investment. Men such as these worked on the brink of bankruptcy, occasionally going out of business and sometimes bouncing back with the initiative mainly resting with the vendor. The 20th century witnessed a variation as land syndicates were formed in order to purchase building land to house the workers of the expanding engineering firms. The Luton Land Company was the best known of these but there were many others including, for example, the Culverdene Estate Company and the Grange Estate Company. The membership of these companies comprised businessmen and Councillors and those who were both. The membership of the Luton Land Company (in 1910) included one timber merchant, one builder, two solicitors, four

*The streets of semi-detached houses built during the 1930s on the western side of the New Bedford Road. Included within the picture are Alexandra Avenue, Blenheim Crescent, Carlton Crescent and Montrose Avenue.*

who were in the straw hat trade, an architect and surveyor (B. B. Franklin, who was involved with many land syndicates), a sewing machine engineer, a broker, a schoolmaster, an auctioneer and two of independent means. Of the above, two, timber merchant Harry Arnold and hat manufacturer Walter Primett, were senior Councillors. Detailed research of the land companies would be welcome as this would shed much light on the method by which Luton grew so rapidly in the first half of the 20th century.

The areas which the land syndicates concentrated upon for development were those which were principally owned by the Crawley family to the north of the town. In the inter-war period the Crawleys sold their holdings in Stopsley, Limbury and Biscot and these areas were swiftly built upon. Luton's population rose dramatically at this time, from 61,342 in 1921 to just under 100,000 by the outbreak of World War Two. With land still abundant houses built in the first half of the 20th century for the most part possessed generous back gardens of at least 50 feet and often a third bedroom, a feature in particular of the increasing number of semi-detached houses.

Amongst those acquiring land was the firm owned by H. C. (later Sir Herbert) Janes and much of this land was to wait until after the easing of building restrictions in the early 1950s before the large estates at Vauxhall Park, Stopsley, Limbury Mead and Sundon Park could be built. This period saw a revolution in home ownership as the proportion of property owners, which had changed little since the late 19th century, increased rapidly. The change can be best illustrated by Janes' own company: between 1919 and 1939 the company built 8,195 houses of which over 40% were purchased by investors to rent out to other people. In just nine years between 1952 and 1960 Janes built 8,525 houses entirely for home owners. Many of those were people buying for the first time, their wages being able to match the mortgage on an affordable Janes house which, although smaller than the standard semi of the time (a downstairs bathroom was a feature), was built upon a sufficiently generous plot of land to allow for extension: something which has subsequently occurred to many of these houses.

*The Janes estate on Limbury Mead.*

By the late 1970s the abundance of land which had been in almost constant supply since the 1830s was beginning to dry up as Luton built almost to the limits of its borough boundary. There was, furthermore, a shortage of public housing and the houses on the Marsh Farm estate which had been built by Janes, soon to be taken over by Barratt Homes, were bought by the Borough Council in order to increase its own housing stock. The 1980s saw the building of the Bramingham estate, the Wigmore estate and the commencement of the Bushmead estate on virtually the last available plots of building ground. Luton's modern history has shown that districts have been developed which are beyond the borough boundary, for example Brown Brick and Sundon Park, to be incorporated within the town at a later date. Should the demand for land for industry and housing continue at the intensity of the last 150 years it is possible that this is the way that Luton's rapacious expansion will continue.

# RELIGION

## The Medieval Era

Throughout the medieval period the Church and the power it wielded pervaded every aspect of the daily life of all sections of the community; furthermore, the Christian faith was accepted without question. The church building provided the focus for many of the town's activities, a central point which all would recognise. It is not known what Luton's church looked like at the time of the Domesday survey, or even where it was located, since early in the 12th century it was demolished and rebuilt on a new site by the Lord of the Manor at that time, the Earl of Gloucester. The building work was completed in 1137 but during the following centuries it was altered, restored and added to many times, until it became one of the largest and finest parish churches in England.

Towards the end of the medieval period, some began to question the power and authority of the Church but it was not until the 16th century Reformation when Henry VIII detached his country's Church from Rome that dissatisfaction found expression in action. The dissolution of the monasteries in 1536–40 affected Luton less than the neighbouring towns of St. Albans and Dunstable, with their great monastic houses, but the Guild of the Holy Trinity was dissolved in 1547 and this may have affected Luton more since so many of the town's leading citizens had been associated with it. However, the Commissioners who wound up the Guild found it in a state of decline; no money had been paid to any poor person from the Guild's funds for the previous five years and its two priests

*A view of St. Mary's Church from the garden of the White House on Park Square, late 19th century.*

were 'meanly learned' and so were pensioned off with £5.00 per year.

## The Rise of Dissent

Although the authorities struggled to maintain a uniformity of belief during the rest of the 16th and early 17th centuries, there was little they could do to turn back the rising tide of dissent. More people were able to read (though not necessarily to write) and more had access to the Bible in English than had previously been the case. Some even owned copies: one such was Edward Ashby, a Luton weaver, who died in 1619; amongst his very meagre possessions was a Bible worth ten shillings (50 pence).

The period of the Civil War and Commonwealth was a time of unprecedented liberty of thought and speech, which saw the establishment of many political and religious movements which hitherto had been only undercurrents in thought and in society as a whole. The freedom of the Commonwealth saw the foundation of many of the county's nonconformist churches but Luton had to wait until almost the end of the century before such a church was set up in the town.

Prior to 1689, the Luton Independents (later known as Baptists) had been part of the flourishing Baptist community at Kensworth but an internal dispute led the Luton members to divide off and form their own church under the leadership of Thomas Marsom, a member of a well established local family of merchants and shopkeepers. The church grew and flourished. Their first meeting house was built at the end of a short alley off Park Street in about 1698. Various pieces of land were added to the site during the 18th century to allow for a burial ground and improvements to the property. Galleries were added to the interior in 1708 and 1774 but these could not cope with the growth in numbers of people attending the church, so it was totally enlarged in 1788, only to be replaced entirely in 1814 with what became known as the Round Meeting, which was capable of holding 800 people.

*The Baptists have had four chapels on their site in Park Street since the 17th century as well as one which was never completed. This was only partially built when it was blown down during a gale in February 1866, destroying the Round Meeting House (pictured here) which was situated alongside.*

Another group of nonconformists with strong roots in the town was the Society of Friends (Quakers); there were members in the town almost from the start of the Society's history. George Fox, its founder, visited the town a number of times and John Crook, whose home near Ridgmont had been the location for the first national gathering (Yearly Meeting) of the Society in 1658, moved to Park Square after his property had been sequestrated following the restoration of the monarchy in 1660.

For nonconformists life after the restoration was very difficult; all those who dissented from the Church of England faced persecution. Toleration came with the accession of William III. In 1676, Luton was estimated to have 70 nonconformists; by 1715, this figure was increased to between 400 and 500, though this includes those from the hamlets and probably some of the surrounding villages as well; people travelled many miles to attend their preferred place of worship.

Although freedom of worship was allowed, political freedom was restricted; excluded from legal and academic professions and from holding public office, many nonconformists used their talents in trade, industry and commerce, gaining influence and power in their communities out of all proportion to their actual number. One particular Quaker family, the Browns, exemplifies this in Luton. For over 200 years members of this family were prominent in different areas of commercial activity in the town and, when restrictions were lifted, were active in philanthropic and public enterprises.

However, nonconformists were very much in the minority in the town in the 17th and early 18th centuries. The majority of people adhered to the Church of England. During the Commonwealth, the vicars had considerable difficulties in maintaining a congregation who were opposed to the new forms of worship without the Prayer Book and one of them, John Jessop, complained to Oliver Cromwell about the 'malignant and prelatical party' against whom he had been struggling. With the restoration of the monarchy, the use of the Prayer Book was reinstated and Thomas Pomfret, who seems to have been much liked in the town, was appointed vicar.

One of the curates at the parish church, Coriolanus Coplestone, appointed in 1771, was an admirer of the evangelical work of John Wesley, the founder of Methodism. Another of Wesley's supporters and friends was William Cole of Sundon. Wesley preached in the parish church a number of times but on his visits to Luton later in the 18th century he was able to preach in a chapel which William Cole had had built, almost exactly opposite the parish church in Church Street. In this way the Methodist Church was established in Luton. By the beginning of the following century it was flourishing to such a degree that a new chapel had to be built for its members in what was later to be called Chapel Street; it was a long way from the harness maker's upstairs room where Wesley preached when he first came to Luton.

*The Wesleyan Chapel in Church Street. The 1851 Religious Census revealed that an average of 43% of Luton's population attended a church.*

## Religious Rivalry

Towards the end of the 18th century, the rise of nonconformity and the decline in the support for the Anglican Church coincided with one another but occurred, in part, for different reasons. Control of the appointment of Vicars to St. Mary's lay with the Lord of the Manor (the Earls and Marquesses of Bute) and the Church of England was to suffer from a series of absentee and short-term incumbents. Charles Henry Hall, Vicar from 1804 until 1827, appears to have rarely set foot in the church after his inaugural service. He was succeeded by a relative of the Marquess of Bute, William MacDouall, who chose to live at Copt Hall and leave all the work to his Curate

Thomas Sikes. MacDouall's most notable reform was to remove the old pews and replace them with new ones which, according to Church historian Henry Cobbe, separated 'the congregation into classes according to their grade in Society', a move guaranteed to have a negative impact in egalitarian Luton. MacDouall remained suspicious of new technology, refusing the introduction of gas lighting and consequently in winter evensong took place in the afternoon. By 1850, St. Mary's had not received the benefit of an active incumbent within living memory and the fabric of the building, as well as the spiritual life of its parishioners, was in a poor state: complaints were made about the state of the graveyard and the poor standard of the singing and music, and the place was described as 'eerie, bleak and desolate'.

In sharp contrast the nonconformist chapels expanded dramatically for most of the 19th century. The natural supporters of the Church of England, the aristocracy, the gentry and the farmers, people who could be relied upon not only to attend Anglican Church but also to encourage and coerce others to do so, were vacating Luton, their place in the town was being taken by people who were drawn to the town by opportunities in business and employment. The virtues which were being promoted from nonconformist chapels at that time such as reliability, sobriety, honesty, hard-work, good stewardship, punctuality and self discipline, were also the values which were most needed and appreciated in Luton's industry. In a town of self-made men and women, the plain, simple theology of the chapels, not least that all were equal in the sight of God (even though the practise of this varied considerably from place to place) carried great appeal. In a town containing so many newcomers, few schools and few places for recreation the chapels possessed other uses. They were a place to make friends, to find a collective identity, to receive the rudiments of learning, to go on outings (also through the Sunday School) and to join clubs: barely a week went by without an event connected with one of the chapels being advertised in the local press. With St. Mary's languishing in utter torpor and neglect the chapels spread, although they

*King Street Congregational Church photographed from a building in Stuart Street soon after its construction in 1866. The Congregational Church was formed after an amicable split from the Union Church in Castle Street; it had a high proportion of Luton's affluent middle class amongst its members.*

*Rev. J. H. Hitchens, a highly successful church builder, flanked by the Deacons of King Street Congregational Church c.1868. Clockwise from the left are: A. T. Webster, George Street hat manufacturer; G. M. Johnson, provision dealer; Charles Robinson, hat manufacturer; W. T. Coates, draper; Hugh Gunn, hat manufacturer; Charles Tomalin, baker. Men such as these formed the leadership of most of Luton's chapels, stamping their personal philosophy upon them in the process.*

too relied heavily upon a successful minister, such as Rev. Wright Shovelton at Chapel Street Wesleyan or Rev. John Jordan Davies at Park Street Baptist. The main appeal of the chapels was directed at the business and artisan classes, two groups which were particularly prominent in Luton.

The consequence of all this was made apparent in the Religious Census of 1851. Whereas in England the respective adherents to the established Church on the one hand and the nonconformist chapels on the other was roughly even, in Luton the ratio was one to three. In fact this could have been even worse for the Church of England had it not been for Rev. Thomas Sikes who had moved from being Curate to Vicar in 1850 and was busily trying both to restore the standing of St.

*St. Mary's Church Choir c.1890. On the left is the formidable bulk of Rev. James O'Neill.*

Mary's and to expand the work of the Anglican Church in the growing town. The bulk of the revival effort, however, came from one of Sikes' later successors, Rev. James O'Neill. In a town noted for its colourful characters, O'Neill stood out as one of the most remarkable of men and certainly there could have been fewer more pugnacious clerics ever to step into a pulpit. To O'Neill goes the credit for the much needed restoration of the fabric of the building and the dramatic improvement in the quality of music in the church. He was also greatly admired by some for his work in the secular arena as a staunch bulwark against the spendthrift inclinations of the liberals, particularly in the field of education where he continued to resist the creation of a School Board, even after it became a *fait accompli.* To others, however, including many Anglicans and Conservatives, O' Neill was nothing more than an odious bully. Amongst the many personal disputes in which he was involved he was sued at least twice by the owner of Stockwood and on one infamous occasion he was charged with assaulting Samuel Oliver, his Churchwarden, the court case deteriorating into farce as O'Neill found himself being simultaneously sued for libel by Oliver's solicitor. Not the least savoury aspect of O'Neill's behaviour was his willingness to tolerate mob rule at public meetings in order to intimidate his opponents and he lost no opportunity to try and undermine the influence of the nonconformists. That the Church of England revived in this period is undeniable but one wonders how much more successful it would have been had it been led by someone less infuriating.

## The 20th Century

O'Neill died in December 1896, aged 76 and still the Vicar of St. Mary's. By this time many of the causes over which he and the nonconformist liberals had done battle were beginning to fade. After 700 years the Christian faith was gradually being separated from the secular world as its involvement in social welfare, education and leisure diminished, its nominal link with local government in Luton having long since disappeared.

*The big chapels in the centre of town put much effort into church planning in the outlying villages and hamlets. A Baptist chapel was established in the remote hamlet of Limbury in 1906 and was sustained in its early years by Park Street Baptist Church.*

With the reasons for going to church becoming more and more simply a matter for those who were believers, attendances also began to fall away, a feature especially felt in the vast 1,000 seaters in the heart of Luton which was, in addition, experiencing a steady depopulation throughout the 20th century. In another respect all denominations continued to expand with the Church of England continually carving out new parishes to fit Luton's expanding urban population and the Baptists, Methodists and Roman Catholics planting new churches in the old villages and new estates of Luton. The nonconformist influence, as well as its conscience, continued to be felt in Luton through the activities of men such as Sir John Burgoyne and Sir Herbert Janes and through the

*Limbury Baptist Church Sunday School outing, 13th June 1918. The Sunday School outing provided many children and adults with a rare chance to travel beyond their immediate locality, even it it was only to a neighbouring county.*

continued reluctance on the part of the magistrates bench to grant new licences to sell alcohol. By the 1970s the various Protestant denominations, at least, were showing a willingness to co-ordinate their church planting activities, for example at Wigmore, thereby avoiding unnecessary duplication of cost and effort. This has been a commendable departure from the bitter inter-denominational wranglings of the 19th century which would have astonished many clergymen of that time and made O'Neill apoplectic with rage.

Congregations have always shown an inclination to move from one church to another and back again according to the appeal of the resident minister. This has continued to be the case with the added factor that the old barriers have steadily been eroded and also, to a certain extent, by differences in style of worship and cross-denominational issues of theology. Luton has always been a town receptive to varied beliefs. In the

*Canon William Davison, Vicar of St. Mary's from 1933 until 1961.*

19th and early 20th centuries this was more usually manifested in an assortment of Christian sects, many short lived and some more than a little odd. In the post-war era the town has witnessed the introduction of new faiths brought in by the more recent immigrants to the town and, of these, Islam has been the largest and most notable. Its influence, although significant, has remained largely within the community of its adherents, mainly of Pakistani and Bengali origin, and it is debatable whether the intensity of this hold will survive the gradual assimilation of subsequent generations of Asians into a secular world which has created its own gods.

# EDUCATION

## Before Local Authorities

It is not known when the first school began in Luton. Before the reformation the monasteries and the church were the main centres of learning but the invention of printing in the 15th century brought books and literacy within reach of many more people. In 1673 Cornelius Bigland, the town's barber surgeon left money 'for clothing, maintaining, schooling and educating six poor children of the town forever.' Twelve years later Roger Gillingham bequeathed £10.00 a year for a schoolmaster to teach 'such poor children of the parish of Luton as shall be nominated by...the lords and owners of the manor house and park of Luton Hoo for the time being.'

In the 18th century other such charitably-minded citizens made bequests for the education of boys in the town (at this time girls were expected to be educated at home) and the wills refer to 'the free school' and 'the church school'. Although it is not altogether certain, it would seem from these references that the school was held in the parish church. The schoolmaster at the end of the 18th century was Joseph Freeman; his death in 1794 was deemed noteworthy, not because of his occupation but because he was the father of thirty four children.

In 1809 a school was built in Park Square on land provided by the Marquess of Bute. It was run on lines put forward by Joseph Lancaster, a prominent Quaker and education reformer. His plan was a very simple one: one qualified teacher could instruct a group of older children, known as monitors, and they in turn would teach the younger pupils. In 1818 it was reported that 135 boys and 135 girls attended the school, the former during the day and the latter in the evening. The same report stated that there were 'six pay schools, three for boys and three for girls, containing altogether 255 children' in the town. These may have been dame schools or boarding schools for the children of middle class parents. The report adds that there were also a number of schools in Luton (including the hamlets) where the children were sent 'for the exclusive purpose of learning straw plaiting, although these seem to have disappeared with the decline of straw plaiting within the town itself.

Most educational efforts at this time left the majority of children, particularly girls, completely untouched. For a variety of reasons connected with its social and economic structure, the south midlands was a region possessing very low standards of literacy with Bedfordshire being its most backward county. Whatever virtues were being displayed in Luton's inexorable growth, erudition most certainly was not one of them: a letter to the *Bedfordshire Times* in 1847 complained that 'bad grammar, bad rhyme and bad taste are simultaneously perpetrated' upon the gravestones in the town. Unfettered enterprise was building Luton and many of those who had come to the town subsequently to enjoy a modicum of success could do so without the benefits of schooling: they may well have come to the conclusion that what had been good enough for them was good enough for other generations. Certainly there was a fear amongst the small manufacturers, builders and shopkeepers about the consequent effect upon local taxes which increased educational provision might bring and so most educational developments in the 19th century were spearheaded by a minority of Lutonians who were usually drawn from the small class of clerics, professionals and larger factory owners. A further complication was added by the inability of the Church of England and the nonconformists to decide where the control of local education should lie.

Schools run on Lancasterian principles were much favoured by nonconformists, since the religious instruction was non-sectarian, but the Park Square school came under the control of the Church of England and the rift between the two elements was deepened in 1835 when a new school was opened in Church Street, the National School, where attendance was limited to those who went to the parish church. The nonconformists raised enough money to build a school in Langley Street; it opened in 1836 with 50 pupils, but before the end of its first year this figure had risen to 150. Daniel Brown, the leading Quaker in the town at that time, personally provided an adjoining school for infants. In addition to this the Wesleyans provided day schooling for between 250 and 300 children adjacent to their church in Chapel Street and at the Crown and Anchor School at the rear of the public house and brewery of the same name in New Bedford Road.

The main thrust of nonconformist effort was made through the Sunday School to which many Lutonians owed the entirety of their educational experience. Laudable though the efforts of

*Langley Street School, opened in 1836, closed in 1964 and demolished five years later.*

*Prayers in an unidentified Sunday School, 1897.*

individual chapels were, the picture by 1870 was of a disorganised assortment of facilities – sectarian, voluntary, charitable and private – which duplicated effort, thereby wasting precious resources and still left an estimated 1200 children completely without schooling. With the advocates of educational provision for all firmly in the minority amongst the ratepaying and, therefore, voting public and with the Vicar of St. Mary's, James O'Neill, determined to control what publicly funded schooling there was, the outlook appeared bleak for Luton's children.

The change came through outside intervention. The Forster

101

Education Act of 1870 piloted through Parliament by William Gladstone's first Liberal government allowed for the election of local School Boards if provision within a district was deemed to be inadequate. A desperate and rather cynical school building programme initiated by O'Neill failed to hoodwink the Government Inspectors whose recommendation for the creation of a School Board was implemented in 1874. Luton became beset with rowdy meetings, protests, handbills, letters to the press and a high level of personal animosity in the build up to the first elections at which O'Neill and his supporters, through sheer incompetence, contrived to turn a natural majority amongst Luton's ratepayers into a defeat at the polls.

## Local Control

The winners of the first School Board election, to become known as the Bible Five, were determined to raise educational standards in the town and were to control the Luton School Board for 21 of the 28 years which it existed. In this time eight schools were built situated at Biscot, Leagrave, Waller Street, Chapel Street, Old Bedford Road, Hitchin Road, Surrey Street and Dunstable Road. Courageously, at a time when child labour was very much in use in the hat trade, attendance at school was made compulsory. Despite a willingness to take legal action against those parents who withheld their children from school, this proved difficult to enforce: the local magistrates were criticised for not being supportive (two of whom had been prominent opponents of the School Board) and, besides the hat trade, there were other distractions which could reduce school attendance including harvest time, Sunday School treats or even the arrival in town of the circus. The religious influence upon Luton's education began to fade during this time.

Lutonians living in the late-19th and 20th centuries were on the whole very much better educated than their forefathers. From the Balfour Education Act of 1902 until Luton became a County Borough in 1964 the town controlled more or less all of its education, although the County Council at various times

The boys of Waller Street School stare confidently back at the camera c.1908. Waller Street was the first purpose-built school constructed in the town following the creation of a School Board. During the 1890s it was the leading boys school in the town.

*Tennyson Road Netball Team, 1926. Walter Haith, Headmaster, is on the left.*

was the principal authority with its power varying from the running of establishments for those over the age of fourteen to the nominal responsibility for all education in Luton. Each change excited fears in the town that hard-earned gains would be sacrificed as a result of a loss of local control but discretionary powers were granted which in practice left plenty of room for local initiatives.

Many local politicians responsible for Luton's schools took a parsimonious approach toward investment in education. On the other hand there was also a succession of Councillors and officers who were influenced by what was once known as the nonconformist conscience and who were committed to the virtues of learning. Of the former group George Warren, a hat manufacturer, a Liberal and Methodist who was born in Barton, was Chairman of the Luton School Board from 1895 until 1903 and, when it was replaced by the Luton Education Committee under the auspices of the Balfour Act, became the chairman of that body until 1914. A later holder of this office for thirteen years was Sir John Burgoyne, who was first elected Chairman in 1938. Burgoyne also originated from one of the

*Sir John Burgoyone, 1875-1969, a popular Mayor of Luton during World War Two, who devoted much of his public career to the improvement of educational opportunities for Lutonians, and never lost a fascination for learning himself. He retained a close involvement with Luton College, enrolling as the 5,000th student for a Methods Engineering Course, student number 6,000 (at the age of 81) for Advanced Bricklaying and student number 7,000 (at the age of 83) for Typewriting.*

villages on the outskirts of Luton (Aley Green) and, like Warren, he was a Methodist and Liberal who made his living in the straw hat trade. Burgoyne, however, retired from business early to embark upon a career in local politics and in particular to pursue a life-long passion for education. Burgoyne served also on the County Education Committee from 1934 and was on the governing body of Luton Grammar School, Luton High School (where the poor level of education for girls was at last being properly redressed) and the Technical College on Park Square. Perhaps the most notable of the officers was Frederick (later Sir Frederick) Mander who was educated at Waller Street School, later becoming headmaster of Hitchin Road School and, upon leaving teaching in Luton, became President and General Secretary of the National Union of Teachers, and Chairman of Bedfordshire County Council from 1952 until 1962.

*Luton Modern School. Established in 1902, this was a co-educational institution until the opening of the Luton High School for girls in 1919.*

For all of Luton's prominence at County Council level, the overall control granted to Bedfordshire by the Butler Education Act of 1944 was irksome to many in the town. Administrative delays were one criticism but no doubt the sheer ignominy of authority being exercised over Luton from Bedford featured strongly. One area where most criticism was levelled at the rural outlook of the County Council was in its inability to understand the importance of technical education, a need felt more acutely by industrial Luton. To redress this the College of Technology was built on Park Square between 1957 and 1960, around the former Modern School which was then demolished. At the same time the Technical School was moved to a new building in New Bedford Road, later being renamed Barnfield College.

The new Luton College of Technology nearing completion in 1956 with the old College building still visible. Costing just under £2,000,000, Luton College grew from 6,000 students in the mid-1950s to 9,000 thirty years later of which 1,100 were full-time. Further expansion in the 1990s outgrew the Park Square buildings to the extent that the College started using a number of sites around the town including those formerly occupied by the Luton News and Hayward Tyler.

The measure of the extent of Luton's practical control over the learning of its young people was that the short-lived County Borough of Luton made little difference to provision in terms of facilities. What it did do, however, was to switch the town's system over to one which was comprehensive and co-educational, the exception to the latter being at Challney. Like most developments in education before and since, this was a controversial move and did not carry the full support of all the authority's officers. Comprehensive education survived the return of power to County Hall under local government re-organisation in 1974 but the relinquishing of control over its schools and colleges was the most controversial of all of Luton's lost powers. Should further change to local government result in Luton becoming a unitary authority, the town is unlikely to regain the influence it once possessed.

*Sports Day at Rotheram High School, 1961. A notable feature of schools built after 1945 was the incorporation of far more extensive playing fields and sporting facilities.*

# WELFARE

## Healthcare

For much of Luton's history, the care of the poor and the sick rested on a combination of self reliance, philanthropy and minimal public support. The inadequacy of this approach necessitated the greater involvement of the state from the 1830s until it became by far the greatest conduit of healthcare and social assistance. In medieval Luton, it was one of the duties of the Church to look after the sick, the poor and the needy but for the majority of people there was little help outside their own homes and family circle. For those without even this means of support, the outlook was dire.

At this time the word 'hospital' meant a place where travellers, especially pilgrims, could stay and rest on their journey. Gradually, however, the care given to travellers was extended to the sick and those in need. In Luton there was such a hospital, with a chapel attached, at Farley. Built soon after 1156, it was run initially by French monks. Over the centuries it acquired considerable amounts of land and property in the area but unlike some hospitals, it did not survive the dissolution of the smaller monastic houses in the reign of Edward VI.

There was another hospital in the area, known as 'The House of God of the Virgin Mary and St. Mary Magdalene'; this was an Augustinian foundation, run by 'brethren and sisters'. It was founded by Thomas à Becket, built near Spittlesea, in the vicinity of the present airport and seems to have been devoted to the care of the sick. Outside the town, probably in the Leagrave/Limbury area, was another hospital or home but this one was for lepers and those suffering from severe skin conditions fostered by the low standard of living and poor diet of the time. However, the surviving evidence for both these hospitals is scant and very little is known about them other than their actual existence. The care which the sick received in these hospitals was probably of the most simple kind; wide use was made of herbs grown in the hospitals' own gardens and bleeding patients was a common, if drastic, remedy. Much greater emphasis was placed on spiritual health.

With the dissolution of the monasteries, what little hospital care there was in the area disappeared. Most families were in any case self-reliant; housewives had their own remedies for minor ailments but more help was available from the 17th century onwards from people such as Cornelius Bigland, barber-surgeon, John Lister, apothecary, or surgeons Thomas Powell and Mr.Kirby. The last named may not have been a popular choice, though, for in 1777 he was described as 'a man of a cruel, arbitrary disposition.' None of his apprentices served out their time with him.

Obstetrics were the preserve of women, usually untrained but not necessarily unskilled midwives. In the 18th century, however, the new profession of 'man-midwife' appears; Samuel Chase of Park Square described himself as such in 1780 and five years later he and his sons were classified as 'apothecaries, men midwives and surgeons.' However, to use the services of such men cost money, but some doctors had contracts with the overseers of the poor, so the very sick and needy did not go entirely unattended.

The Luton Union workhouse contained not only the destitute but also the sick, infirm and 'lunatics'. Unwilling or unable to pay for a full-time Medical Officer, the Board of Guardians engaged a local doctor in a part-time capacity instead. E. O. Woakes and later Kit Tomson were the first two holders of this post but no matter how conscientious they were, and Tomson was particularly energetic, their other medical commitments meant that they were only able to offer limited assistance. This left care to the Master and other staff whose abilities were at best rudimentary: fever swept through the workhouse in the summer of 1847 and amongst those who died was the Master himself. Several changes followed: the addition of an infirmary including the removal of children to a new hospital in London Road in 1894, thanks to the generosity of a retired hat manufacturer, A. P. Welch, the appointment in 1927 of a full-time nurse and in 1929 a change of name to St. Mary's Hospital when the Board of Guardians was replaced as the administering authority by the County Council. These developments, however, did little to alleviate the institution's dismal reputation. Most people had to rely principally upon self-help for health care, leaving the poor and ill-informed particularly prey to unsuitable medicines, sometimes peddled at market by quacks but also widely available at corner shops and chemists: for example, there are numerous instances of death to young infants being caused through being given 'Godfrey's Cordial', a lethal opium based sedative, by mothers who were anxious to quieten their fractious offspring.

It was the admirable Dr. Woakes who pioneered Luton's first public hospital. The Luton Cottage Hospital contained a handful of beds and was situated in High Town Road. It was a charitable venture supported by members of Luton's middle class whose philanthropy was co-ordinated by Woakes and a Management Committee. Aimed at the 'artisan class', patients were expected to contribute around half the cost of their treatment. The success of the cottage hospital necessitated expansion of the service and in 1882 it was superseded by a new hospital next door to the workhouse in Dunstable Road. Known simply as 'the Bute' this initially contained 20 beds but was expanded, including the addition of a casualty department, to meet Luton's rapidly rising population. The Bute was funded on similar lines to the Cottage Hospital and the Children's Hospital, being supported through a variety of fund raising methods and fees from patients according to their ability to pay. A private wing in Grove Road was also added. To deal with epidemics of infectious diseases, which mainly afflicted children, an Isolation Hospital was opened at Spittlesea on the eastern edge of town in 1892 and a Smallpox Hospital was later added nearby.

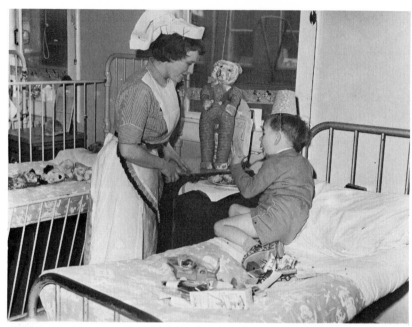

*Christmas time at the Children's Hospital in London Road, 1958.
Dr Horace Sworder was the first Medical Superintendent. Like other
medical establishments the Children's Hospital used a number of
methods for raising funds to support its running costs including, for
example, the endowment of cots and the staging of Garment Days and
Egg Weeks.*

Like the Cottage Hospital, the Bute was outgrown by the
town it sought to serve, by the increasing requirements of
medical technology and the demands of its patients. A
programme to raise £100,000 was launched towards a
hospital, provisionally entitled the New Bute Hospital, to be
built at Lewsey Farm. Erected by H. C. Janes, the new building
was opened by Queen Mary on 14th January, 1939 and was
instead known as the Luton and Dunstable Hospital (or more
simply 'the L and D'). Lawrence Plewes had the honour of
becoming Luton's first full-time consultant, the number of
which increased with the creation of the National Health
Service in 1948 and the subsequent expansion of patient care.
This has led to extensions covering the whole Lewsey site so

that the original buildings can now barely be seen. The work of the various outstations has gradually been drawn into the L and D: Spittlesea, thankfully less needed, closed in 1968; the former Children's Hospital, later annexe, closed in 1983 and the last patients from St. Mary's were transferred in 1991. In the same year, a specialist area of care which could not be met so well by the L and D, that for the terminally ill, was met by the opening of a hospice at Bramingham, the costs of its construction being raised by the people in the locality which it will serve.

*Luton and Dunstable Hospital in the summer of 1953.*

## Social Welfare

In a sequence of events similar to healthcare, the assistance given to the poor by the Church and organisations such as the Guild of the Holy Trinity, became greatly diminished upon the dissolution of the monasteries and many became dependent upon the charity of individuals rather than institutions. Until the end of the 16th century there was little attempt to organise such help but a series of disastrous harvests in the 1590s, a recurrence of plague in some parts of the country and an escalating problem of unemployment and poverty forced the government to act.

The Poor Laws of 1597–1601 consolidated previous attempts to cope with the problem of the poor, and the system which evolved lasted until the early 19th century. The parish, as a civil rather than ecclesiastical unit of government, became responsible for the poor, the sick, the unemployed and those who were otherwise in need; Overseers, appointed by the Justices of the Peace, were empowered to assess and levy poor rates in order to fund whatever measures were deemed necessary to solve the problem.

One method which many parishes used was to adapt an existing building or build a workhouse where the poor and needy could be housed, cared for and provided with work. The regime in many workhouses left much to be desired; unfortunately very little is known about the one in Luton. According to Frederick Davis the first workhouse was located in the buildings of the Langley Mansion House which was situated in Castle Street. In 1724 it was reported as being an old commodious building with room for about 80 people. It was described as the House of Maintenance for the Poor in order to 'soften the appellation of workhouse, against which the poor might be prejudiced'; there were 20 adults and 20 children in it at that time, 'lodged and dieted in a clean, wholesome manner.'

Later in the 18th century the parish used a building next to the Tithe Barn in Park Street as a workhouse; the building was extended and two adjoining cottages were added to it but by 1835 the accommodation provided there was described as 'very limited.' In the following year, one of the first acts of the newly appointed Board of Guardians was to have a new, much larger workhouse built in Dunstable Road. The old workhouse was converted back into cottages.

Public provision such as this left plenty of room for additional private philanthropy. For example, in the early 17th century Robert Napier and Edward Vaughan provided almshouses on Tower Hill (Manchester Street) for 'poor widows and other poor persons.' There were several such charitable endowments in the town, some for the benefit of the needy, others to provide education or apprenticeships. Most of these charities were administered by the parish; others, such as the Hibbert Charity, were controlled by private trustees. The Hibbert Charity was founded by Robert Hibbert who lived at The Hyde; much of his wealth came from sugar plantations in Jamaica. His philanthropy was widespread, but in 1819 he gave a row of cottages in Castle Street for the accommodation of 24 poor widows; he also provided sufficient funds for the maintenance and repair of the cottages or almshouses as they were known. They were later relocated to the appropriately named Hibbert Street. In 1853 an investigating committee of Luton businessmen was set up by a vestry meeting to look into the way that the charities money was being administered by the parish over the previous sixteen years. Its grim report concluded that because of the 'inefficient manner' in which the charities were being run 'several hundreds of pounds have been lost to the poor of this parish'.

The Elizabethan Poor Laws, based upon the parish, were reckoned to be financially too weak and inefficient to cope with the rising number of poverty stricken individuals and families who increased total national expenditure on poor relief by between two and three times during the Napoleonic Wars and the years of depression and political turmoil which followed it. The Poor Law Amendment Act of 1834 was a first significant intrusion by central government into the administration of localities grouping the 15,000 parishes in England and Wales into large Unions each centred upon a 'deterrent' workhouse to be used by the impoverished as a last, desperate resort. The new Luton Union covered not only the town and its hamlets but also most of the parishes of southern Bedfordshire (including Dunstable) in which administration of poor relief was now the responsibility of elected Guardians from each parish who were empowered to make such appointments to alleviate distress as were deemed necessary. This meant not

*Luton Union Workhouse photographed c.1906.*

only the staff who administered the workhouse but also overseers responsible for giving outdoor relief.

Luton's straw hat trade, although never free from the prospect of depression, offered markedly better prospects for young people in particular than that which existed in the rural backwater of Bedfordshire. Strong family ties, the cornerstone of self-help, were bound to be weaker in a place with so many newcomers. There were certainly many in the town who lived in a degree of poverty which it is difficult to imagine today and during slack periods and depressions in the hat trade this would be especially marked. This problem would be counterbalanced by the high proportion of migratory labour who simply left the town when the hat trade's busy season ended in May. Certainly Luton's workhouse, described as a 'miserable pauper prison' would have been turned to only as a last resort as would have been the Relieving Officer, Charles Maffey, who was eventually forced to resign in 1870 over his 'harsh and oppressive treatment of the poor'. 'The Poor Law....is little else than a mockery in Luton' commented the *Luton Times* in 1867. The philanthropic outlets of the numerous chapels were a far more effective mechanism for assistance and, although trade unionism came late to Luton, branches of Friendly Societies such as the Oddfellows and the Foresters were formed around the 1840s: by 1859 the oldest Oddfellows lodge had 202 members supporting 60 widows and 40 orphans.

The introduction of national welfare reforms by Herbert Asquith, David Lloyd George and Winston Churchill in 1908-11, developed further in the years after World War Two, asserted to an even greater degree control by central government over people's well being, diminishing local and individual responsibilities in the process. Already by this time Luton had done much itself. Although the Board of Guardians was inadequate the two principal local authorities, the Board of Health (1850-1876) and the Borough Council (from 1876), had done much to improve the living environment of Lutonians. After an inauspicious start the Board of Health succeeded in ensuring that all houses were constructed to a sound and healthy standard although they were less successful in regulating the number of people who crammed into them during the height of the hat season. In 1856 the plight of one man and his family was highlighted by the local press: arriving late at night they made their way to a lodging house in New Town where they were shown to their small room; in addition to the vermin in it, there were two beds, a bedstead and already seventeen other occupants.

The Borough of Luton possessed far more extensive powers, progressively being able to extend its functions to cover, by 1934, all areas of sanitary inspection as well as maternity and childcare. The sewage works, dreadfully mismanaged in the mid-19th century by men with a closer eye upon that day's rates rather than long term costs and health care, were improved by the Borough and a new sewage disposal plant was opened at East Hyde in 1942. Although fortunate in being a town built upon industrial wealth, Luton has never had full

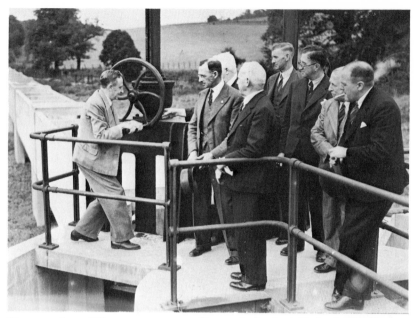

*The opening of the new sewage disposal plant at Hyde in September 1942. The disposal of Luton's waste had been a particular problem for the town. The preferred option of the 1850s, allowing the River Lea to carry it away, lasted until the local authority was sued by the owner of Luton Hoo (through whose park the river travelled) necessitating the building of the first sewage plant at the Brache in 1856. This was succeeded by plant near Eaton Green Road in 1886.*

control over the welfare of its citizens, increasingly becoming reliant upon direct agencies of central government and also having to share such functions with County Council administration. This latter relationship has not worked to the full satisfaction of Lutonians, many of whom felt that the county lagged behind the town in developments of social welfare and even hindered Luton in its own ambitions.

# TIME OFF

## The Market Town

Leisure is closely linked with the nature of a local economy and until the late 19th century opportunities for relaxation for ordinary Lutonians were few and far between. Indeed, in the 15th and 16th centuries many sports and games were forbidden by law, which, of course, implies that they were being played. Top spinning, for example, a popular adult

*A market on Park Square in 1906. Street fairs and markets were a regular feature of Luton life from the founding of the town until 1929.*

activity at the time, was forbidden in Luton in 1528; the authorities considered that time would be better devoted to learning, not playing. The punishment for spinning tops was a day and a night in the stocks. For many centuries Luton was principally a market town and this was reflected in the type of entertainment that was enjoyed. The Statute ('Stattie') Fair held in September for the purpose of the hiring of workers for the coming agricultural year was also a major festival of entertainment. A newspaper report from 1850 described some the attractions on offer: '...tall men, fat women, peep shows, ginger bread, and oysters...conjurors, pugilists and negro melodists. We regret to say...that the light fingered gentry were very busy in their avocations and reaped a rich harvest'. There was also an April Fair, which later took the name of the 'Stattie', and the Fox Fair. Other visiting entertainments, such as Wombwell's Menagerie, would lodge themselves in convenient fields on the outskirts of the small town. Horse racing would also take place on the outskirts and as early as 1247 'the whole countryside met at the chapel of Limbury for sports.' Unfortunately it was not an enjoyable occasion for all, since a scuffle broke out and one of the participants was killed.

The main focus of regular entertainment for many hundreds of years was the public house. Aside from the regular enticement of a degree of warmth, comfort and conviviality which may not be available in the home, the main public houses were the sites for travelling entertainments: for example, visiting theatrical companies used the Red Lion on Market Hill. The Soaksters Club was formed in the early 19th century, holding its meetings at The Dog tavern in Castle Street. It devoted its evenings to serious drinking and possessed just one rule: no 'low quarrelling'.

## The Religious Influence

During the medieval period the festivals of the church were the main holidays. Fairs took place on religious holidays and the one held each August would have been a high point for many people, with its entertainers, music and visitors from far afield.

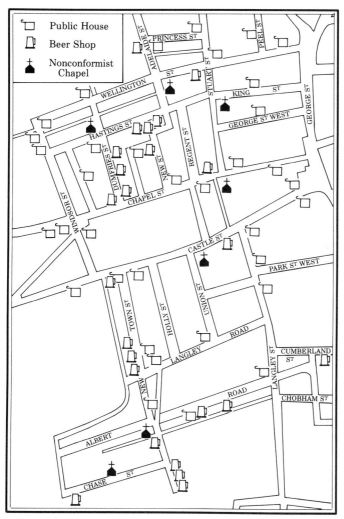

*Pub and pulpit: the distribution of public houses, beer shops and chapels in New Town c.1865. There was also a successful 'Wooden Church' run independently of St. Mary's by an Anglican vicar but the effort of the main nonconformist chapels in the poorest streets was restricted to mission halls run by a few hardy souls. One worker associated with the Chase Street Mission recalled that 'the work was hard and very rough . . . those who attended having the freest idea as to their liberty of speech and conduct'. (Drawn by Jo Richards.)*

Guy Fawkes night was a popular festival with religious overtones but was a spontaneous occasion with fireworks let off in the street, thus making it a rather hazardous entertainment. As Luton ceased to be a market town in the 19th century, its traditional, rustic and rough forms of entertainment came to be viewed in a different light by the sober, chapel going section of the population which were building the town. The fairs were regarded as a source of drunkenness, petty theft, prostitution and violence, whilst Guy Fawkes night was seen as an excuse for minor acts of arson. Of the 'Stattie' fairs the Luton Times wrote in 1858: 'they form a nucleus for the assembling together...of the lowest orders; they seduce by their excitement and glitter, hundreds of the lowly born from a regular and honest course of living: they are a means of organising systematic robberies and fraud from the same class, and they bring with them pollution and vice wherever they are suffered to take place'. The public houses were regarded in the same hostile light as the fairs with the added condemnation that some of the worst were no more than fronts for all manners of criminal activity: commenting on the Elephant and Castle in Church Street, Inspector James of the Luton Police stated that he 'had never seen a respectable person in it'.

The chapels sought to provide an alternative forum of entertainment to lure people away from the temptation of pub and beershop. Luton's earliest picture shows were provided by the magic lantern (an early slide projector) and these were usually held in church halls, carrying a powerful religious message. From the Sunday School came the annual outing to a nearby beauty spot, a day which provided many Lutonians with their only holiday, and many churches provided further outings through their temperance organisations. Both the magic lantern and the Sunday School outing were further developed by an enterprising Baptist and teetotaller, T. G. Hobbs. A keen photographer, Hobbs wrote his own slide illustrated talk set in Luton, which told the downfall of a fictitious hat manufacturer through drink. At the turn of the century he would deliver this, together with other lectures, to

*The forlorn figure of Margaret Wilson, one who found no fortune in Luton. A 23 year old widow, standing just four feet eight and a half inches, she tramped from St. Albans to Luton in June 1866 dressed 'in the most wretched attire' at a time when the hat trade was buoyant, although at the end of its busy season. She was convicted of breaking a window and sentenced to a fine of 10 shillings (50 pence: more than a week's wage) or ten days imprisonment. Upon conviction she was taken to the cells whereupon she immediately broke another eight windows, was at once returned to the dock and promptly given six weeks' hard labour. (Produced with permission of Bedfordshire Record Office.)*

audiences of hundreds of people in the Plait Halls. Hobbs also developed the Sunday School outing into tours which took people to the coast, to the Lake District and, more ambitiously, to the continent.

Prominent amongst the regular societies which based themselves within chapels were those devoted to music. Choral societies and brass bands were popular and from these stemmed two of Luton's most notable contributions to the cultural life of the country. The Luton Red Cross Band (later just the Luton Band) was originally based at the Ashton Street Mission. After steadily building a formidable reputation it achieved the ultimate accolade when in 1923, under the

*The climax of T. G. Hobbs' fictitious temperance lecture* Sewing and Sowing: *a drunk and incapable Mr Smythe is returned home ot the tradesman's entrance of his house supported by the strong arm of the law. Within 48 hours he died from alcohol poisoning.*

guidance of Fred Mortimer, it became the first and only southern band to win the National Championships at Crystal Palace. From Ceylon Baptist Church in the 1930s came a choir created by Arthur E. Davies which which was to earn even greater renown than the Luton Band. Arguably, the Luton Girls Choir did more to promote the name of the town at home and abroad than did any other of its exports, including hats and cars. Arthur E. Davies was an accomplished pianist and conductor of the Luton Choral Society but his great love was

*The world's best brass band, the Luton's Red Cross Band, pose proudly before the entrance to Wardown House after winning the championship in 1923.*

the choir of his creation which he ruled over with kindness and good humour. Good voices, Davies believed, were a gift from God and as such should be encouraged to develop to the full in the happiest of atmospheres. The Luton Girls Choir effectively died with Davies in 1976.

Churches provided patronage to amateur dramatic groups such as the St. Christopher's Players (formed in 1946) and the St. Andrew's Players (1952). Secular organisations such as the Luton Harmonic Society and the Luton Choral Society were led and filled by people whose musical abilities and oratorical skills were developed through church activities. The various organisations of church life, not least the Pleasant Sunday Afternoon, encouraged many individuals' enjoyment of leisure, providing them with opportunities which they would not otherwise have enjoyed.

## The Secular World

In 1871 Henry Wright, headmaster and later to be Mayor, observed that there was nothing to do in Luton between 'pub and pulpit'. This complaint, echoed many times down subsequent years, was an exaggeration which still contained a germ of accuracy. Many of Britain's towns and cities possessed powerful middle classes, large businesses, public schools or local authorities which could provide the organisation and facilities for leisure. Apart from the bigger hat factories such as Vyse's, which organised annual outings and cricket matches for its employees, Luton had none of these. The small workshops, builder's yards and corner shops which characterised the town worked the sort of hours which allowed little time for leisure: during the hat trades' busy season many worked as long as they could and when the season ended many simply left the town. After 1855, the overall standard of housing was good but Luton was never an attractive town and for many years largely bereft of cultural facilities. It was not, therefore, surprising that many people, working long hours and who in many cases would be newcomers to the place, would look to their home and family as the main source of relaxation after work was over. The Lutonian's traditional obsession with domestic virtues did not find favour with everyone from outside the town – a woman from London's East End who was evacuated with her family in 1939 was heard to complain: 'Heaven preserve me from ever becoming like Lutonians. I never met such a snobbish, selfish, unfriendly, rude lot in all my life. All they think about is their homes. House-proud, that's their trouble'.

Henry Wright's complaint was made just as the secular world was beginning to make its presence felt in the world of leisure. In 1869 the Board of Health prompted the building of the Plait Halls and the Corn Exchange, two years earlier Luton acquired Peoples Park through an exchange of land with the Crawleys and in 1872 public baths were built in Waller Street. The nature of the town's industries were also beginning to change from this time with the accelerating arrival of new

*The elegant interior of the Palace Theatre, built in 1912. It was later converted into the Majestic Ballroom and finally into a bingo hall. It was destroyed by fire in 1982.*

127

engineering firms and the gradual replacement of the plethora of small hat workshops with fewer and larger concerns. This factor had a two-fold change on the way in which Lutonians could spend their time off. First it provided an increasing number of workers with regular hours of employment and, therefore, fixed time off, with the weekend starting at Saturday lunchtime. The establishment of a vast number of sporting sides between 1880 and 1910, of which Luton Town Football Club (1885) was by far the most important, is testimony to this. Theatres were also being established with the Alexandra (1880) preceding the Grand (1898), a theatre capable of seating nearly a thousand people, and the Palace (1912). Greater literacy brought about by Luton's belated improvement in educational standards saw the establishment of a public

*The Charlton Athletic goalkeeper intercepts the ball ahead of the predatory approach of Gordon Turner, taken in 1963 during Luton's plummet down the leagues which saw the club slide from the First to the Fourth Divisions in little over five years. From its earliest days a feature of Luton Town's history has been the need to offset lower than average gates by selling players.*

library in 1883, containing an embryonic museum, which was replaced by the elegant Carnegie Library in 1910.

The second way in which Luton's economic change provided new outlets for leisure was through the new firms themselves. Vauxhall's extensive social and sporting organisations have already been noted and they covered almost every conceivable field. In addition to the flourishing, and in some cases highly accomplished sports clubs, drama and music were both supported with concerts being held in the large canteen hall. SKF, Kent's and, to lesser degrees, the other engineering firms in the town also possessed highly organised and active social clubs.

## The 20th Century

The Borough Council was beginning to find its feet in the 20th century: in 1905, after some prompting from Asher Hucklesby, Edwin and Albert Oakley, three of its most powerful members, the Council resolved to purchase Wardown, a park then on the northern outskirts of the town. Spruced up with an extended boating lake, additional tennis courts, bowling greens, drinking fountain and a bandstand, Wardown outshone the other parks in the town becoming the focal point for the social life of most Lutonians, particularly on summer weekends. Not least of the attractions associated with Wardown was the 'Monkey Parade', a promenade of young people dressed up in their best clothes and strolling from the town centre along the New Bedford Road to the park. How many Luton marriages were the result of introductions made at the 'Monkey Parade' it is impossible to tell, but there must have been many.

Two years after opening the Carnegie Library the Council virtually rebuilt the baths on their same site in Waller Street. The swimming pool was used in the summer but covered over in the autumn to become the Winter Assembly Hall and used for meetings and dances. The lack of a purpose-built assembly hall became more keenly felt as the various old halls which were capable of holding large audiences – namely the Palace, the Grand, the big cinemas, the market halls, the Corn

*Wardown Park in the 1950s, a photograph probably taken at the time of the Easter Bonnet Parade as a catwalk has been laid out from the bandstand. Wardown, its house, lodges, park, lake and cricket ground, cost the Council £16,250 to purchase. a bargain price in 1905.*

*The dance floor of the Winter Assembly Hall in Waller Street being taken up in March 1954 for conversion into Luton's main indoor swimming pool, the building's summer time use. The Assembly Hall/Swimming Pool was built in 1913.*

Exchange and the Winter Assembly Hall itself – were all demolished. A plan to place a large assembly hall to the rear of the new Town Hall when it was being built in 1936 was abandoned through lack of money and from that time numerous schemes for a civic centre have been mooted but have never reached fruition. It is debatable whether there exists a sufficient demand for such a building.

When in 1931 the Council voted to move Luton Museum from the Carnegie Library to the then redundant mansion in Wardown Park one member, Councillor Mitchell, spoke up in opposition stating that what Luton required was more emphasis given to sporting and outdoor recreation facilities. The second part of Councillor Mitchell's wish was achieved as

*Wardown House, photographed c.1913 by W. H. Cox. Built in two stages during the 1860s and 1870s for local solicitor F. C. Scargill, the name of the house and surrounding estate was Bramingham Shot. After acquisition by the Council it was used as flats for employees and also contained a tea room. Luton Museum moved into Wardown House in 1931.*

the town expanded: parks and recreation grounds were steadily added, not least the 265 acre (107 hectare) Stockwood Park which was acquired after the last of the Crawleys moved out. With so much provided by company social clubs progress on the development of purpose built leisure centres remained slow until the 1970s, with the notable exception of facilities for swimming: the open air swimming pool (1935) was joined by 30 years later by a large indoor pool on an adjacent site. The shift in emphasis was formalised with the changing of the Borough's Parks and Cemeteries Department to the Recreation Services Department (now Leisure and Amenities Department) in 1974. A flurry of building was already under way, with a

*The opening of the open air swimming pool alongside what became Bath Road in 1935. Originally, there was changing room accommodation for 900 bathers and there were also five diving boards, two shutes and a paddling pool. The main pool had a capacity of 448,000 gallons. Irretrievable cracking in the pool lining resulted in its closure in 1989.*

succession of community and sports centres being established, and these were to a large extent filling the gap left by the gradual decline in the strength of the industrial sports and social clubs.

It is generally acknowledged that the 20th century has witnessed an increase in the amount of time available for people in Britain to spend at their leisure. The forms of recreation in each locality remains as closely tied to the way in which people work as it ever did and for much of the 20th century many Lutonians countered the increased free time by extending their working day through overtime and putting the benefits of this into to their homes. In the 1990s Lutonians have never had a broader range of ways from which to choose to spend their leisure time but whilst it is likely that the overall amount of this time will continue to grow, there is also the possibility that a steady divergence in incomes could mean that Lutonians will spend this time in very different ways. Luton has never been attractive to tourists and the facilities which it possessed served the indigenous population. The more affluent and mobile will have the opportunity to enjoy not only the full range of facilities locally but also those further afield. Others will be obliged to look closer to home and should the cost of leisure become prohibitive, the public house and the church may yet again come into their own.

# LOCAL GOVERNMENT AND POLITICS

## National Politics and Local Allegiances

At the time of the Domesday Survey Luton was a royal manor. It remained the monarch's land until the early 12th century when, on a number of occasions, it passed between the Crown and relations or favourites of the King. Stephen granted it to one of his favourites, Robert de Waudari, who built a castle (after which Castle Street is named) in 1139. Of simple construction, comprising a wooden building on a mound with a defended yard, it would have been easy to dismantle in 1154 when de Waudari was banished. The following year the manor reverted to the Crown.

In the early 13th century the manor came into the possession of Falkes de Breauté, one of King John's favourites and regarded by some as an unscrupulous freebooter. He built a castle near the parish church and in 1221 he dammed the river, making it overflow onto church lands, flooding homes and preventing the abbot's mill from grinding corn. His violence and the widespread disruption that he caused was his undoing; he was eventually banished and the King once again repossessed the manor.

Later, many of the county's estates were divided up and smaller manors began to emerge. In 1274 the manor of Luton was split into six and by 1400 the town and its hamlets consisted of over 30 manors, reflecting the number of landowning families. In the 15th and 16th centuries these families tended to consolidate their holdings and some of them, such as the Crawleys, come to the forefront.

Some members of these families took part in national affairs and events, such as the Hundred Years War with France and the Wars of the Roses. Sir Thomas Hoo of Luton Hoo and Sir John Wenlock of Someries both saw service in France, and Sir John was active in the Wars of the Roses. At first he supported the Lancastrian cause but then switched to the Yorkist side. He was killed in action at the battle of Tewkesbury in 1471.

Nearly 200 years later another civil war ravaged the country. From the outbreak of war in 1642, Bedfordshire was within the Parliamentary area and the county was a member of the Midland Association. Many of the county's representatives in London were active Parliamentarians and many members of the local gentry held important commands in the two opposing armies.

Recruiting men for military service met with opposition; even when recruits were raised, they frequently deserted. Even more unpopular were attempts to raise money, especially if the cause was a remote one, such as the maintenance of the army in Ireland. The presence of the parliamentary forces seems to have been as objectionable to local people as was that of the royalists. The commandeering of supplies, the taking of horses and wagons as well as quartering of soldiers, were particular causes of complaint in an area dependent on the annual cycle of seed time and harvest.

No major engagements were fought in the county but there were numerous minor incidents. In August 1645 the King passed through the county on his way to Oxford; there was fighting on Bedford bridge and a detachment of royalists plundered Luton, though they were attacked and defeated by a force from Markyate. There was another short encounter in 1648 when a considerable royalist force passed through Luton during the last phases of the war.

The 18th century was the last era in which the aristocracy were in a position to dominate local politics. In 1763 Luton Hoo was purchased by John, third Earl of Bute, who was Prime Minister from 1762–63. Bute, however, was preferring to concentrate his activities locally in establishing the Hoo as a

136

centre for works of art, botany and books and Luton was just one small town within the larger Bedfordshire constituency. County politics from the latter part of the century were dominated by the Whigs through the Russells, Dukes of Bedford at Woburn and the Whitbread family.

From the ending of the Napoleonic Wars until after World War One urban Liberalism was the predominant political force within Luton. In every parliamentary election Luton voted heavily Liberal, sometimes in a ratio over the Conservative vote of three to one. The Conservative Party did not win Luton until 1922 and the Labour Party was not successful in returning an M. P. (and gaining control of the Council) until 1945.

There were numerous reasons for this Liberal allegiance. In an era when the Tories nationally were the party associated with tariffs, Luton by contrast was a town being built from the mid-19th century upon free trade, a commitment shared by the evolving Liberal Party of whom, nationally, William Gladstone was becoming by far the dominant figure. Luton's numerous small businesses, whether they were drapers, millers or hat manufacturers, all possessed a vested interest in keeping protectionism to the minimum; and many of them were also beneficiaries from the extension of the suffrage in 1832. After the failure of Chartism in the 1840s it was these groups which formed the backbone of the national Liberal Party. The local allegiance to Liberalism was given sharper focus by the absence of the sources of serious rivalry. The bastions of old Tory patronage, namely the aristocracy, the farming interest and the Church of England declined along with the market town, whilst the selling off of the Bute estate for building reduced its influence still further, at the same time contributing to the free market industrialisation of Luton. St. Mary's was also administered indifferently and this further assisted the flourishing of the theological ally of the Liberals, the nonconformist chapels. Neither were Luton's industries suited to the development of organised labour, the rise of which in parts of Britain pushed the shopkeepers and small manufacturers into the waiting embrace of the Conservative Party far sooner than happened in Luton.

It is possible to overstate Luton's Liberalism. Because it was so dominant and also because in many respects Luton was a politically-neutered town, subject to Bedford, there was little point in fierce party rivalry for the control of local institutions. Issues of debate in the town frequently crossed party lines. Liberals and Conservatives worked in alliance with one another in campaigning for a Board of Health or a School Board and were themselves opposed by other Liberals and Conservatives. Luton Liberals often showed a marked preference for Luton Conservatives rather than for the Bedfordshire Whigs (the Liberal ally and begetter nationally) dominated by the patronage of the Russells. For example, had J. G. Leigh, a man with little to commend him locally other than that he owned Luton Hoo, been selected for the 1872 Bedfordshire by-election by the Conservatives instead of Captain Stuart there is little doubt that Luton's voters would have switched votes in sufficient number to lose the election for the Liberals.

Luton was a town filling rapidly with migrants, many of whom were escaping the backwardness, squalor and, in some cases, the oppression of a rural England dominated by the Tory squires and farmers. They came to a town which was being built with no aristocracy, no powerful large manufacturers and no influential clergy jealously guarding its privileges but instead where political and economic liberty was held to be of great importance and where rural values counted for nothing. This mixture of free trade, radicalism and nonconformity were each contributing to a distinctive Luton character. Viewed from the sedate county town and its satellite villages, Luton soon became regarded as a brash, dirty town where rioting was commonplace (then as now an exaggeration), where people were uncouth and not as deferential as they ought to be.

A residue of that simplistic assessment of Luton has lingered on into the 20th century. The town has continued to attract migrant workers but the political consequences, in terms of party support, has altered. Following the decline of Liberalism after World War One, the Luton constituency became now more of a barometer of British politics, with one

*Dr Leslie Burgin, the last Liberal M.P. for Luton (he later became a National Liberal) and the first Luton M.P. to become a member of the Cabinet when Neville Chamberlain made him Minister of Supply in July 1939. Burgin did not serve under Churchill and did not fight the 1945 General Election.*

party moving into the ascendant in accordance with the wider fortunes of their national colleagues. Thus Dr. Leslie Burgin, the last Liberal to represent Luton, held his seat from 1931 as a National Liberal, with the support of the Conservatives. Dr. Charles Hill regained Luton for the Conservatives in 1950, a year ahead of their return to power at Westminster and, upon his dropping from the Cabinet and elevation to the Lords, the victory of Will Howie for Labour at an important by-election in 1963 was read by political pundits as heralding the ending of the Conservative government. In more recent times the Luton South seat, encompassing most of the town, has been the one which reflects national politics. It was won by Graham Bright in 1979 (as Luton East) for the Conservatives at a General Election in which Margaret Thatcher came to power. At the 1983 General Election the Conservative majority nationally and locally was increased still further and was reduced again

*Dr Charles Hill was already a nationally known figure as the 'Radio Doctor' and through his involvement with the British Medical Association before he became M.P. for Luton in 1950. He retained his seat at three successive elections and was a member of the Cabinet under Harold Macmillan. Following his elevation to the House of Lords in 1963 he took the title of Lord Hill of Luton.*

in 1987. In 1992, Graham Bright won Luton for a fourth successive time, to the surprise of many, at a time when the Conservative Party confounded political commentatators and the opinion polls by winning an outright victory at the General Election.

## Local Administration

A powerful undercurrent of Luton's modern political history has been its desire to assert itself as a distinctive, independent town. Although this has not always been clearly expressed it has often become focused on Luton's relationship with rural Bedfordshire and its county town. This relationship has not been satisfactory for many Lutonians who have resented the control over its affairs exerted by Bedford, with which it had and still has little in common, coupled with what was regarded as the poor performance of Bedford-based institutions and the fact that Luton ratepayers have had to pay for this privilege. Arguably, this general issue of self-determination, whether expressed through a threat not to pay rates to the county in 1820, or through the issue of control of Luton Airport in the 1990s, has been stronger than any party political allegiance. Luton has always depended, however, upon central government for the extension or curtailment of its powers.

Until the end of the 16th century, the town had been administered by the manors and their courts, sometimes known as court leets. Although the manor and the landowning families remained an influence in the town, their power was decreasing. From the beginning of the 17th century much of Luton's day to day government was in the hands of the Vestry Meeting. This was a meeting of the chief ratepayers in the town; the meeting was summoned by the churchwardens and had a variety of powers, including the right to appoint local constables and overseers. The overseers were responsible for the welfare of those in need as well as seeing that the roads and paths were maintained and sewage and rubbish removed.

The Vestry proved to be one of Luton's most durable institutions: even into the first third of the 19th century it attracted a large proportion of the town's most important citizens to its deliberations and the role of chairman as well as the office of churchwarden were still positions commanding respect. Like so much else in Luton, however, the Vestry was rendered obsolete by the transformation of the town from the 1830s onward. The evaporation of the power of the Anglican Church due to internal neglect and the rise of nonconformity meant that the levying of the Church Rate, the main responsibility of the Churchwarden, was abandoned after the 1830s when the nonconformists in Luton simply refused to pay it. The successive creation of the Board of Guardians,

Board of Health and Borough Council trimmed the remnant of its secular responsibilities, leaving the Vestry by the 1870s with little else other than ecclesiastical matters to concern itself with and, since the Vicar of Luton rarely bothered to attend, the chairmanship of its meetings was often taken by non-Anglicans. At this time public meetings were still referred to as Vestry Meetings.

The demise of the Vestry was an experience which it shared with many other local institutions. As Luton's relentless development continued, bodies which had once been central to the life of the town dwindled into the background. Often instead of summary abolition they were left to linger on, like

*The most distinctive sight on the streets of Luton during the first part of the 20th century was that of Charlie Irons, the Town Crier. He was recalled as being 'over six feet tall, a green top hat accentuated his height, with wax moustaches, far reaching' and also possessing a 'foghorn of a voice'. This photograph was taken on Park Square, two doors down from the Modern School.*

ghosts from a bygone era, going through the motions of authority whilst effective power was being wielded elsewhere. The Court Leet continued to meet until 1939 and the office of Town Crier survived principally out of sympathy for the ageing Charlie Irons, the last holder of this office, until his death in 1941. The Board of Guardians, an institution which served a substantial proportion of southern Bedfordshire as well as Luton, was consequently never regarded as an adequately representative institution for the town. Whereas elsewhere in England control of the Board of Guardians (as well as the office of Churchwarden) was an issue of heated local debate, in-fighting and corruption, in Luton the Board was just a backwater (with notable exceptions) for the lightweight, the incompetent and the infirm. The Board of Health began life in 1850 with vitriolic battles amongst the leading farmers, professionals and manufacturers for control of what was described as the 'little parliament in Stuart Street'. Twenty years later the local press was able to comment about the annual elections that 'no more interest was taken in the Board of Health elections last year than in the selection of an errand boy or washerwoman'.

Part of the problem was local control. Much of Luton's affairs in the 19th century, including those of the Vestry and the Board of Health, were under the control the Quarter Sessions held at Bedford and also the weekly magistrates courts. This 'degrading' situation was made worse by the fact that it was not until 1868 that a Lutonian was entrusted with the position of magistrate and the assortment of rural clergy and squires who were supposed to do the job failed in that position, with the honourable exception of Col. Lionel Ames of the Hyde. On more than one occasion no magistrate turned up and the sitting had to be postponed.

In the opinion of a number of Lutonians the solution was to establish the town as a parliamentary borough, separate from the rest of the county. When this failed twice in the 1860s the town then settled for status as a municipal borough in a move which was shrewdly spearheaded by William Bigg. The granting of this did not greatly increase the degree of control

*Some of the members of Luton Council stand assertively before the camera in 1894. In the front are Edwin Oakley (with brother Albert immediately behind), Asher J. Hucklesby and Town Clerk, George Sell. Between Oakley and Hucklesby is George Warren and directly above Hucklesby is Henry Blundell. Peering over Blundell's left shoulder is Albert Wilkinson, the manager of Hucklesby's hat factory. Men such as these wielded a decisive influence over most aspects of local life.*

which Luton would be able to exercise over its own affairs, except in policing and the local administration of justice, and it is fair to say that most Lutonians were indifferent toward this achievement. This fact was born out both by the poor turnout at the first borough elections in May 1876 at which, incidentally, women voted for the first time and also the slightly odd assortment of candidates who were successful in becoming councillors. It was only as the fledgeling Corporation consolidated its authority over the next fifteen years that the principal manufacturers in the town were attracted to serve upon the Borough Council.

With the exception of the years 1964–74, the period between 1890 and 1945 was the era in which Luton's control over its own affairs was at its zenith, even allowing for the failure of Luton to obtain County Borough status in 1914. Through a combination of the Corporation, the Chamber of Commerce, the New Industries Committee, the Local Education Authority and the various land syndicates the town controlled virtually all aspects of its development which mattered. In every area of local life, from schooling through to jobs, sanitation, housing, recreation and the supply of both water and power, Lutonians experienced improvement in their lives, improvements which were in no small measure due to the activities of their local institutions. In 1898 the Town Clerk, George Sell, had asserted in relation to the development of towns that 'the only question worth talking about is main roads, and the rest does not matter'. Forty years later the Corporation was looking even further forward, or rather upward: it opened Luton Airport.

The old Luton tradition of disregard of authority lingered into the 20th century, manifesting itself in 1919 when a crowd, furious at the mishandling of the celebrations to commemorate the ending of World War One, ransacked and burnt down the Town Hall. At the same time the Council became more politicised, with party group discipline making it far harder for some individuals to merge the public interest with personal benefit. During World War Two the Mayor of Luton, John (later Sir John) Burgoyne probably exercised greater authority over

145

*Luton Airport was created by the Corporation and opened on 16th July 1938. Since that time the Council has continued to provide the necessary investment and support. A concrete runway was not installed until 1959 but in the decade which followed, Luton Airport benefitted from the expansion in package tours which necessitated a succession of improvements to its facilities, including new terminal buildings in 1966 and 1984. (This photograph by Bob Irons shows grounded Court Line aircraft following the collapse of the company in 1974.)*

the town than any of his predecessors or successors in that office. Proud of its performance during the war the Borough Council commissioned the Report on Luton in 1945 as a preparation for the expansion of public services to meet perceived needs in housing, education, health and industry. It recognised the 'interdependence of town and county' but also emphasised, with an unmistakable note of regret that over half the rates levied in Luton were spent by the County Council and that whilst the rateable value of the rest of Bedfordshire had increased by 30% between 1901–43, in the corresponding period Luton's had increased by 408%.

The post-war re-organisation of local government was consequently a disappointment to many in Luton. Having had

*A photograph taken at the moment that Luton's Peace Day celebrations on 19th July 1919 began to go awry. A crowd of Lutonians, angry at the way that Luton Council had organised the preparations for the celebrations to mark the end of World War One, charged toward the Mayor during the main parade in George Street, forcing him to flee within the Town Hall. A handful of police were left to try and appease the crowd.*

control over its education placed under the nominal administration of the County in 1944, this was followed three years later by the loss of the fire and police services to the County Council. Some Luton members of the County Council were criticised for 'going county', not for the first time, failing to represent properly the interests of the industrial town within the rural shire with which it felt it had little in common except, in the areas bordering the town, as possible future sites for housing and business development. The solution, elevation of Luton to the status of County Borough, was pursued several times during the 1950s but fell on the floor of the House of Commons. It was not until 1964 that County Borough status was granted whereby Luton retrieved the functions which it had lost previously.

That County Borough status lasted only ten years before local government reorganisation again swept powers back to Bedford was, and remains, a matter of regret for some in Luton. In truth, national trends had already rendered obsolete the old parochial rivalries between Luton and Bedfordshire. Control of public transport, gas, water and electricity had ceased to be a matter for either Town Hall or County Hall by 1974 and for much of the 20th century central government has become more and more involved in nearly all aspects of the life of the individual. In particular, since the mid 1970s the degree of financial control exercised by successive Secretaries of State for the Environment over local government has increased noticeably. This has now reached the stage whereby traditional areas of local authority responsibility, notably health and education, are now moving toward direct funding from, and therefore subservience to, Whitehall. Whatever functions Luton will be granted in the future its dominant relationship will not be with Bedford but with central government and this relationship is unlikely to be an equal one.

# A SELECTION OF FURTHER READING

## Books about Luton

Andrews, William. *Illustrated History of Luton and District Brass Bands* (Town and Country Press, 1907).

Austin, Thomas George. *The Straw Trade* (Patrick O'Doherty, 1871).

Austin, William. *The History of Luton and its Hamlets, vols. I and II* (The County Press, 1928).

Austin, William. *Fifty Years of Freemasonry in Luton* (Alfred Atkins, 1891).

Balch, Rev. A. Ernest. *A Century of Methodism in Luton* (1908).

Baker, Lionel. *The Story of Luton and its Public Libraries* (Beds County Library and Luton Museum).

Blundell Bros. *Diamond Jubilee of an Enterprising Firm, 1852-1912* (1912).

Borough of Luton, Architects Department. *The Town Hall Clock* (1989).

Bunker, Stephen. *North Chilterns Camera. The Thurston Collection in Luton Museum* (Book Castle, 1989).

Clarke, Dorothy *et al. Thirty Years of Progress. Short History and Directory of the Trade Union Movement in Luton and District* (Luton, Dunstable and District Trades Council, 1941).

Cobbe, Henry. *Luton Church* (George Bell and Sons, 1899).

Collings, Harry. *History of Union Chapel* (Samuel Pride, 1887).

Collings, Timothy. *The Luton Town Story 1885-1985* (Luton Town Football and Athletic Co. Ltd.).

Cooper, Ken. *Luton Scene Again* (Phillimore, 1990).

Currie, Margaret. *Hospitals in Luton and Dunstable. An Illustrated History* (1982).

Darby, Aubrey S. *A View from the Alley* (Luton Museum, 1974).

Davis, Frederick. *The History of Luton* (John Wiseman, 1855).

Davis, Frederick. *Luton, Past and Present* (Stalker, 1874).

Dony, J. G. *A History of Education in Luton* (Luton Museum, 1970).

Dony, J. G. *A History of the Straw Hat Industry* (Gibbs, Bamforth & Co., 1942).

Dony, J. G. *et al. The Story of High Town* (Beds County Library, 1984).

Dony, J. G. and Dyer, James. *The Story of Luton* (White Crescent Press, 3rd edition, 1975).

Dyer, James. *The Story of the Stopsley Schools* (Luton Museum, 1989).

Ellis, Geoff et al. Blenheim Crescent Baptist Church. The First Fifty Years (1987).

Fisher, J. S. People of the Meeting House (Park Street Baptist Church, 1975).

Fletcher, G. Impact! An Outline of Luton Methodism (1962).

Freeman, Charles. Luton and the Hat Industry (Luton Museum, 1953).

Freeman, Charles. The Romance of the Straw Hat (Luton Museum, 1933).

George Kent Ltd. The George Kent Centenary (1938).

Glass, Jamie. The Story of Luton International Airport (Published by the author and Luton International Airport, 1988).

Grundy, Fred and Titmuss, Richard M. Report on Luton (Gibbs, Bamforth and Co., 1945).

Hambermehl, Rev. K. C. The Story of Christ Church, Luton (1956).

Hawkes, Joseph. The Rise and Progress of the Wesleyan Sunday Schools, Luton. (A. J. Giles, 1885).

Higgins, D. M. Old Luton (Scientific, Literary and Artistic Club, Luton, 1885).

Hobbs, T. G. Luton and Neighbourhood Illustrated (T. G. Hobbs, 1908).

Hobbs, T. G. Recollections of Early Luton (Reprinted from the Luton News, 1933).

Inwards, Harry. Straw Hats: their history and manufacture (Isaac Pitman & Sons, 1922).

Kingham, J. A. South Beds. Golf Club: the First 100 Years 1892–1992 (South Beds. Golf Club, 1992).

Luton Adult School Jubilee Souvenir 1862–1912 (1912).

Luton Choral Society. Centenary 1871–1970 (1970).

Luton Gas Company. 100 Years of Service (1934).

Luton Industrial Co-operative Society Ltd. Our Fifty Years of Co-operation (1933).

Luton News. Luton at War (Home Counties Newspapers, 1947, reprinted by Beds. County Library, 1982).

Luton News. Thirty Years of Progress 1891–1921 (Gibbs, Bamforth & Co., 1921).

Mahon, E. B. The Congregational Church.... (Town and County Press, 1914).

New Industries Committee. Luton as An Industrial Centre (Borough of Luton and Luton Chamber of Commerce, 1905).

Peaple, C. J. The Blockers' Seaside. A Selective History of Leagrave (1979).

Saint Peter's Church. A 'Home-made' Church (1914).

Shelbourn, J. E. *St. Matthews, Luton 1876-1976* (1976).

Silvester, R. John. *Percival and Hunting Aircraft* (published by the author, 1987).

SKF. *A Factory Went to War.*

SKF. *Forty Years of Progress* (SKF, 1950).

*Souvenir of the Luton Girls Choir* (c. 1950).

Spedding, Robert K. *'The Hill of the Lord'...High Town Primitive Methodist Church 1838-1932* (1933).

Trevelyan, Raleigh. *Grand Dukes and Diamonds. The Wernhers of Luton Hoo.* (Secker and Warburg, 1991).

Vauxhall Motors Ltd., Public Affairs Dept. *The Griffin Story. A Pictorial History of Vauxhall Cars and Bedford Commercial Vehicles* (1990).

Vigor, Peter. *Memories are Made of This* (Luton Museum, 1983).

Webb, Jack. *A History of Luton Town Cricket Club, 1905-1980* (Luton Town Cricket Club, 1980).

White, Harold (ed.). *Luton Past and Present* (White Crescent Press, 1977).

Workers Educational Association. *Blockers, Boaters and Boots: 50 Years of High Town* (Beds. Leisure Services, 1984).

# Unpublished Writings on Luton

Borough of Luton, Dept. of Planning and Engineering. Economic Development Strategy 1992/93.

Bunker, Stephen. 'Strawopolis'. The Transformation of Luton 1840–1876. Ph.D thesis, *University College London,* 1991.

Dony, J. G. Nuffield College Social Reconstruction Survey. Report on Luton Hat Industry, May 1943.

Dony, J. G. Notes on the Labour Conditions in the Luton Hat Industry (n.d.).

Freeman, Charles. The History of Luton. A course of three lectures given by C. E. Freeman, Curator of Luton Museum, Winter 1957.

Holden, Len. Vauxhall Motors, Luton. (Two volume typescript held at Beds. County Record Office.)

Horsler, George. The Baptists of Limbury (1981).

Kennett, David H. Luton: A Centenary History (1976).

Metcalf, S. The Provision of Parks in 19th Century Britain. IV 1.6 Benefactors: Luton (People's Park). M.A. thesis, *University of London.*

Moore, Valerie J. The families of the Browns and Greens of Luton 1700–1950. Unpublished dissertation, *Putteridge Bury College* (1970).

O'Donoghue, K. The Saxon Cemetery of Luton, Bedfordshire. Unpublished B.A. dissertation, *University of London* (1980).

Parker, R. and M. H. The Story of Our Church 1887 - 1982 (St. Andrews).

Waller, A. E. Albert Road – Some Recollections (1970).

# Information on Luton Contained in other Books and Journals

Bagshawe, T. W. *Basket Making in Bedfordshire* (Luton Museum, 1981).

Branigan, K. *The Catuvellauni* (Alan Sutton Publishing Ltd., 1985).

Bell, Patricia L. *Belief in Bedfordshire* (Belfry Press, 1986).

Burnett, John. *Useful Toil. Autobiographies of Working People from the 1820s to the 1920s.* Part One, Lucy Luck, straw-plait worker and Rosina Wyatt, munitions factory worker.

Chambers, Betty. *Printed Maps and Town Plans of Bedfordshire 1576-1900* (Bedfordshire Historical Record Society, 1983).

Cirket, A. F. The 1830 riots in Bedfordshire, background and events. *Worthington George Smith and Other Studies. Presented to Joyce Godber* (Bedfordshire Historical Society, 1978).

Cockman, F. G. *The Railway Age in Bedfordshire* (Bedfordshire Historical Record Society, 1974).

Cox, Alan. *Survey of Bedfordshire. Brickmaking. A History and Gazetteer* (Beds. County Council and Royal Commission on Historical Monuments, 1979).

Dony, J. G. The 1919 Peace Riots in Luton. *Worthington George Smith and Other Studies. Presented to Joyce Godber* (Bedfordshire Historical Record Society, 1978).

Dyer, J. F. Dray's Ditches, Bedfordshire, and Early Iron Age Territorial Boundaries in the Eastern Chilterns. *Antiquaries Journal* 41 (1961), 32-43.

Dyer, J. F. A Secondary Neolithic Camp at Waulud's Bank, Leagrave. *Bedfordshire Archaeological Journal* 2 (1964), 1-15.

Dyer, J. F. The Excavation of Two Barrows on Galley Hill, Streatley. *Bedfordshire Archaeological Journal* 9 (1974), 13-34.

Dyer, J. F. The Bedfordshire Region in the first Millennium B.C. *Bedfordshire Archaeological Journal* 11 (1976), 7-18.

Hagen, R. Anglo Saxon Burials from the vicinity of Biscot Mill, Luton. *Bedfordshire Archaeological Journal* 6 (1971), 23-6.

Holgate, Robin (ed.). *Archaeology of the Chilterns* (Luton Museum Service, 1993).

Lord Hill of Luton. *Both Sides of the Hill* (Heinemann, 1964).

Holden, Len. 'Think of Me Simply as the Skipper'. Industrial Relations at Vauxhalls 1920–1950. Oral History. *The Journal of the Oral History Society* 9, (2), Autumn 1981.

Howes, Hugh. *Bedfordshire Mills* (Beds. County Planning Dept., 1983).

Matthews, C. L. and Schneider, J. P. *Ancient Dunstable* (2nd edition, 1989).

Mortimer, Harry. *On Brass* (Alphabooks, 1981).

Peck, G. *Bedfordshire Cinemas* (Beds. County Council, 1981).

Silverman, H. A. *Studies in Industrial Organization* (Methuen & Co., 1946). Chapter 4, The Hat Industry by J. G. Dony.

Simco, A. *Survey of Bedfordshire: the Roman Period* (Beds. County Council and Royal Commission on Historical Monuments, 1984).

Smith, Terence Paul. A Demolished Timber-Framed Building at Luton. *Bedfordshire Archaeological Journal* 7, 1972 73–7.

Turner, Graham. *The Car Makers* section II, chapter 2, The Turnip Patch: Industrial Relations at Vauxhall (Eyre and Spottiswoode, 1963).

Turner, H. A. *et al. Labour Relations in the Motor Industry* (George Allen and Unwin Ltd., 1967).

Warburton, Philip. *Treasure in Earthen Vessels. The Story of the Old Baptist Union* (c.1977).

Woodward, G. and S. *The Hatfield, Luton and Dunstable Railway (and on to Leighton Buzzard)* (The Oakwood Press, 1977).

# Leaflets

*The Baptists in Luton* (Luton Museum Service).

*Exploring Luton's Past: archaeological sites to visit in the Luton district* (Luton Museum Service).

*The General Cemetery* (Luton Museum Service).

*A Historical Guide to Luton Museum* (Luton Museum Service).

*Luton and the Society of Friends* (Luton Museum Service).

*Luton Theatres* (Luton Museum Service).

*A Museum for Luton* (Luton Museum Service).

*Stockwood* (Luton Museum Service).

*Underneath the Arndale* (Luton Historical Society and Luton Museum Service).

*Waulud's Bank. The 'Capital' of the Chilterns over 4,000 Years Ago* (Luton Museum Service).

# INDEX

154

# Books Published by THE BOOK CASTLE

**CHANGES IN OUR LANDSCAPE: ASPECTS OF BEDFORDSHIRE, BUCKINGHAMSHIRE and the CHILTERNS, 1947–1992**: from the photographic work of Eric Meadows. 350+ fascinating colour and monochrome pictures by the area's leading landscape photographer. Detailed introduction and captions.

**JOURNEYS INTO HERTFORDSHIRE**: Anthony Mackay. Foreword by The Marquess of Salisbury, Hatfield House. Nearly 200 superbly detailed ink drawings depict the towns, buildings and landscape of this still predominantly rural county.

**JOURNEYS INTO BEDFORDSHIRE**: Anthony Mackay. Foreword by The Marquess of Tavistock, Woburn Abbey. A lavish book of over 150 evocative ink drawings.

**NORTH CHILTERNS CAMERA, 1863–1954: FROM THE THURSTON COLLECTION IN LUTON MUSEUM**: edited by Stephen Bunker. Rural landscapes, town views, studio pictures and unique royal portraits by the area's leading early photographer.

**LEAFING THROUGH LITERATURE: WRITERS' LIVES IN HERTFORDSHIRE AND BEDFORDSHIRE**: David Carroll. Illustrated short biographies of many famous authors and their connections with these counties.

**THROUGH VISITORS' EYES: A BEDFORDSHIRE ANTHOLOGY**: edited by Simon Houfe. Impressions of the county by famous visitors over the last four centuries, thematically arranged and illustrated with line drawings.

**THE HILL OF THE MARTYR: AN ARCHITECTURAL HISTORY OF ST. ALBANS ABBEY**: Eileen Roberts. Scholarly and readable chronological narrative history of Hertfordshire and Bedfordshire's famous cathedral. Fully illustrated with photographs and plans.

**ECHOES: TALES and LEGENDS of BEDFORDSHIRE and HERTFORDSHIRE**: Vic Lea. Thirty, compulsively retold historical incidents.

**LOCAL WALKS: SOUTH BEDFORDSHIRE and NORTH CHILTERNS**: Vaughan Basham. Twenty-seven thematic circular walks.

**CHILTERN WALKS: BUCKINGHAMSHIRE**: Nick Moon. In association with the Chiltern Society, one of a series of three guides to the whole Chilterns. Thirty circular walks.

**CHILTERN WALKS: OXFORDSHIRE and WEST BUCKINGHAMSHIRE**: Nick Moon. In association with the Chiltern Society, another book of thirty circular walks.

**CHILTERN WALKS: HERTFORDSHIRE, BEDFORDSHIRE and NORTH BUCKINGHAMSHIRE**: Nick Moon. Completes the trilogy of circular walks, in association with the Chiltern Society.

**COUNTRY AIR: SUMMER and AUTUMN**: Ron Wilson. The Radio Northampton presenter looks month by month at the countryside's wildlife, customs and lore.

**COUNTRY AIR: WINTER and SPRING**: Ron Wilson. This companion volume completes the year in the countryside.

**WHIPSNADE WILD ANIMAL PARK: 'MY AFRICA'**: Lucy Pendar. Foreword by Andrew Forbes. Introduction by Gerald Durrell. Inside story of sixty years of the Park's animals and people – full of anecdotes, photographs and drawings.

**FARM OF MY CHILDHOOD, 1925–1947**: Mary Roberts. An almost vanished lifestyle on a remote farm near Flitwick.

**SWANS IN MY KITCHEN: The Story of a Swan Sanctuary**: Lis Dorer. Foreword by Dr Philip Burton. Tales of her dedication to the survival of these beautiful birds through her sanctuary near Hemel Hempstead.

**A LASTING IMPRESSION**: Michael Dundrow. An East End boy's wartime experiences as an evacuee on a Chilterns farm at Totternhoe.

**EVA'S STORY: CHESHAM SINCE the TURN of the CENTURY**: Eva Rance. The ever-changing twentieth-century, especially the early years at her parents' general stores, Tebby's, in the High Street.

**DUNSTABLE DECADE: THE EIGHTIES: – A Collection of Photographs**: Pat Lovering. A souvenir book of nearly 300 pictures of people and events in the 1980s.

**DUNSTABLE IN DETAIL**: Nigel Benson. A hundred of the town's buildings and features, plus town trail map.

**OLD DUNSTABLE**: Bill Twaddle. A new edition of this collection of early photographs.

**BOURNE AND BRED: A DUNSTABLE BOYHOOD BETWEEN THE WARS**: Colin Bourne. An elegantly written, well-illustrated book capturing the spirit of the town over fifty years ago.

**ROYAL HOUGHTON**: Pat Lovering. Illustrated history of Houghton Regis from the earliest times to the present.

**THE CHANGING FACE OF LUTON: An Illustrated History**: Stephen Bunker, Robin Holgate and Marian Nichols. Luton's development from earliest times to the present busy industrial town. Illustrated in colour and monchrome. The three authors from Luton Museum are allexperts in local history, archaeology, crafts and social history.

# Related 1993 Titles

**BETWEEN THE HILLS: The Story of Lilley, a Chiltern Village:**
Roy Pinnock. A classic English village between Luton and Hitchin, typical and yet unique, a priceless piece of our heritage. Much of the rural beauty still remains, but the way of life, the superstitions, customs and beliefs described here have largely disappeared. Fascinating photographs too. Author lived in Lilley for nearly fifty years.

**THE MEN WHO WORE STRAW HELMETS: The Luton Borough Police Force 1876–1947: The Luton County Borough Police Force 1964–1966**: Tom Madigan. The meticulously chronicled history of Luton's Police from the early nineteenth century to recent times. All the events and changes are covered chronologically, and general police procedures, legislation and specialist sections are thoroughly discussed. Dozens of rare photographs throughout; full lists of all serving policemen to 1947. The author followed his father into the police and himself served for nearly 50 years.

**LEGACIES: Tales of Luton and the North Chilterns**: Vic Lea.
From the author of Echoes, another lively collection of mysteries and stories based on fact. The material is wide-ranging, but special sections include events at Luton Airport and Luton Town Football Club. Photographs throughout.

# Specially for Children

**ADVENTURE ON THE KNOLLS: A STORY OF IRON AGE BRITAIN**:
Michael Dundrow. Excitement on Totternhoe Knolls as ten-year-old John finds himself back in those dangerous times, confronting Julius Caesar and his army.

**THE RAVENS: ONE BOY AGAINST THE MIGHT OF ROME:**
James Dyer. On the Barton hills and in the south-east of England as the men of the great fort of Ravensburgh (near Hexton) confront the invaders.

Further titles are in preparation.
All the above are available via any bookshop, or from the publisher and bookseller

## THE BOOK CASTLE
### 12 Church Street, Dunstable, Bedfordshire, LU5 4RU
### Tel: (0582) 605670